THE KING'S COMMISSIONERS

For Max, the Math Wizard, and Bess, our
Commissioner for Infinite Energy. —*Aunt Aileen*

For my sister, L.E., Royal Organizer extraordinaire.
—*Susan Guevara*

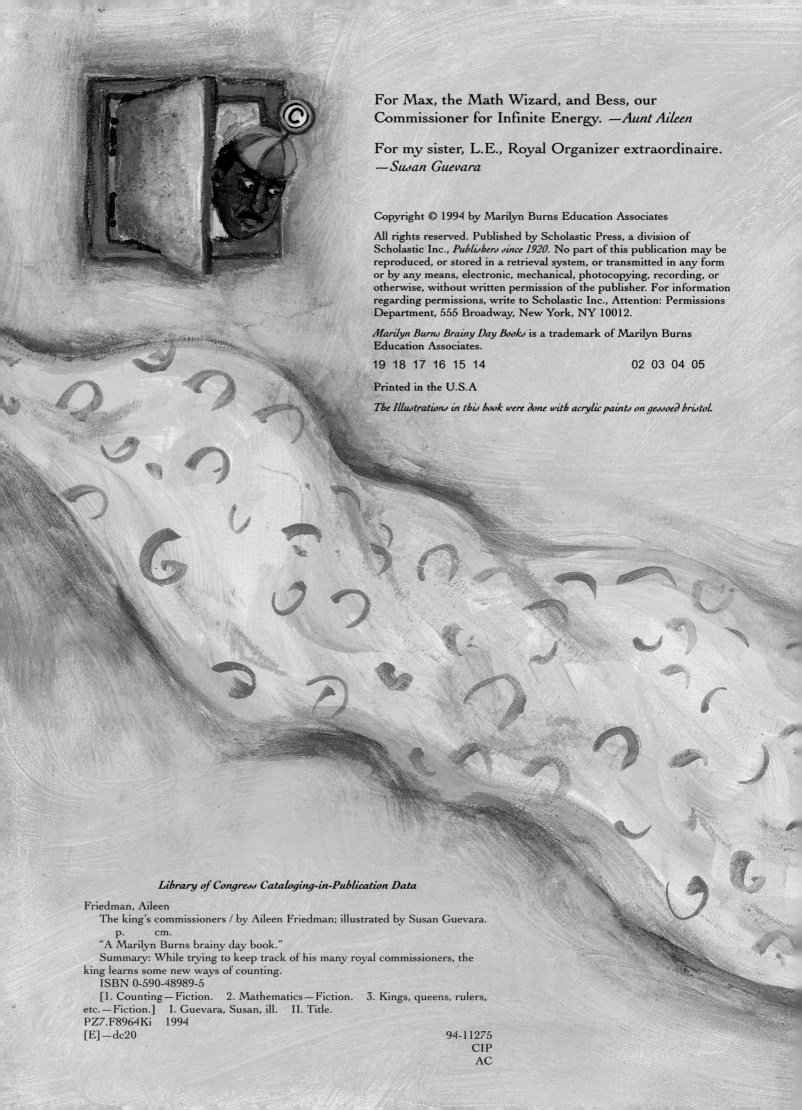

For Max, the Math Wizard, and Bess, our
Commissioner for Infinite Energy. —*Aunt Aileen*

For my sister, L.E., Royal Organizer extraordinaire.
—*Susan Guevara*

Copyright © 1994 by Marilyn Burns Education Associates

Marilyn Burns Brainy Day Books is a trademark of Marilyn Burns
Education Associates.

19 18 17 16 15 14   02 03 04 05

Printed in the U.S.A

The Illustrations in this book were done with acrylic paints on gessoed bristol.

Library of Congress Cataloging-in-Publication Data

Friedman, Aileen
     The king's commissioners / by Aileen Friedman; illustrated by Susan Guevara.
          p.   cm.
     "A Marilyn Burns brainy day book."
     Summary: While trying to keep track of his many royal commissioners, the
king learns some new ways of counting.
     ISBN 0-590-48989-5
     [1. Counting—Fiction.   2. Mathematics—Fiction.   3. Kings, queens, rulers,
etc.—Fiction.]   I. Guevara, Susan, ill.   II. Title.
PZ7.F8964Ki   1994
[E]—dc20
                                          94-11275
                                             CIP
                                             AC

THE KING'S COMMISSIONERS

story *by* Aileen Friedman
pictures by Susan Guevara

A Marilyn Burns Brainy Day Book
Scholastic Inc. • New York

The King was confused.

Every time a problem occurred in his kingdom, the King had appointed a royal commissioner to take care of it.

There was a Commissioner for Flat Tires, one for Chicken Pox, another for Foul Balls. There was even a Commissioner for Things That Go Bump in the Night. This last commissioner had been appointed when the Princess was having scary nightmares.

Now there were so many royal commissioners, the King had lost track of who was taking care of what. He didn't even know how many commissioners he had altogether.

"I've got to get organized!" he thought.

"Well," he thought again, "at least I have to count them."

The King called in his most important helpers, the First Royal Advisor and the Second Royal Advisor.

"We must count all the royal commissioners," the King told them. "I want you to issue an official proclamation. Tell the commissioners to line up outside the throne room tomorrow at three o'clock. And be sure to use all the trumpets we've got."

"How do you plan to count them, Your Majesty?" asked the First Royal Advisor.

"Simple," answered the King. "I'll count them one by one as they come in the door. And just to be sure we get the right number, you and the Second Royal Advisor will count them, too."

The King's advisors did as they were told. The next day at three o'clock a crowd of royal commissioners waited patiently outside the throne room door.

"Okay, it's time," said the King to the First and Second Royal Advisors. "I'll sit here on my throne. One of you stand on the right side of the door and the other stand on the left. Each of us will count."

The Royal Advisors took their places. The King motioned to the Imperial Doorman. "Let in the royal commissioners," he ordered. "One by one."

First came the Commissioner for Spilt Milk. He'd been very busy when the Princess was a baby. The Commissioner for Lost Homework followed. She was very busy now. The Commissioner for Mismatched Socks was next. Then the Commissioner for Wrong Turns.

As the royal commissioners filed into the throne room, the King counted them one by one in his head—1, 2, 3, 4. The Royal Advisors busily made tallies on their large notepads.

Just as the King got to 18, the Princess came running through the royal back door to the throne room. She climbed up on her father's knee and kissed him on the cheek.

As always, the King was delighted to see his daughter. "Hello, my Princess," he said, hugging her tight. "After we finish counting the royal commissioners, you'll tell me about your day at school."

But when the King turned back to the line of commissioners filing into the throne room, he realized that he'd lost count. "No matter," he thought, "my Royal Advisors are counting them as well."

When the last commissioner had filed into the room—the Commissioner for Late Arrivals—the King turned to the First Royal Advisor. "How many commissioners do we have altogether?" he asked.

"Well, Your Highness," said the First Royal Advisor, "I made a tally mark for each commissioner who came in and then circled the marks in 2's." He showed the King his notepad. "There are twenty-three 2's and 1 more…"

"That doesn't tell me anything!" said the King. "I want to know how many commissioners we have altogether."

"But Your Excellency, let me explain. You see…"

The Princess jumped off her father's knee and chimed in. "Yes, Daddy," she said. "He's right…"

But the King ignored them both and motioned for the Second Royal Advisor. "How many commissioners did you count altogether?" the King asked him.

"Well, Your Majesty," the Second Royal Advisor said a little nervously, "I also made a tally mark for each commissioner, but I put the marks in groups of 5." He showed his tally marks to the King. "I got nine 5's and 2 more and that…"

"Stop!" cried the King. "That doesn't tell me anything, either. What I want to know is how many commissioners there are altogether."

"But, sir, I can..." tried the Second Royal Advisor.

"Let me, Daddy, let me," pleaded the Princess.

The King looked down at his eager daughter and sighed. "All right, my dear. You may as well try."

"First, can the Royal Organizer put all the commissioners in rows?" asked the Princess. "Tell him to put 10 commissioners in each row. Then I can count them."

The King sighed again. "I don't know how that will help, but, okay."

Following the King's orders, the Royal Organizer arranged the commissioners in rows of 10. There were four rows and 7 commissioners left over.

The Princess stood in front of the first row of commissioners. "10," she said. Then she walked to the second row. "20," she said next. Walking along the rows, she continued to count. "30. 40. Plus 7 more makes 47."

gene mutations known to cause the disease a person has, but this has been shown to be a poor predictor. Even different patients who have the most common gene mutation have vastly different survival rates. Researchers are currently trying to link other factors to longevity to help with such predictions and to aid in developing new types of therapies.

The most promising methods of achieving an actual cure for CF lie with using gene therapy to correct the genetic defects that cause the disease. Although technical and safety challenges with gene therapy exist, experts are hopeful that this type of cure will someday allow the many patients whose lives have been extended by modern therapies to finally be free of CF. In the meantime, new and better treatments continue to increase the number of people with CF who live active, productive lives that extend further and further into adulthood.

CHAPTER ONE

What Is Cystic Fibrosis?

As the most common fatal genetic disease in the United States and Europe, CF affects about thirty thousand people in America and seventy thousand worldwide. Persons in all racial and ethnic groups get CF, but Caucasians are most often affected. Ashkenazi Jews, whose ancestors came from eastern Europe, are one subgroup of Caucasians that CF most commonly impacts. About 1 in 2,300 Ashkenazi Jews, 1 in 2,500 Caucasian Americans of all ethnicities, 1 in 13,500 Hispanic Americans, 1 in 15,100 African Americans, and 1 in 31,000 Asian Americans have CF.

Medical historians believe CF has affected humans for about fifty thousand years, but the earliest known written references date to European folklore from the Middle Ages. One such reference states, "Woe is the child who tastes salty from a kiss on the brow, for he is cursed, and soon must die."[5] Prior to 1900 salty-tasting skin was the most prominent symptom associated with what was later named cystic fibrosis. Around this time, doctors began to report that many babies and children with salty-tasting skin did not grow normally and had ongoing intestinal upsets and the swollen abdomen that signifies malnutrition. Other doctors noticed that some babies with salty-tasting skin had chronic (ongoing) lung infections, but no one recognized that these diverse symptoms were part of a single disorder until 1938, when Dorothy Andersen published the first description and named the disease.

Relating the Diverse Symptoms

Andersen studied many cases of infants and children with a combination of breathing and digestive problems. She also performed autopsies on those who died from these problems and found fluid-filled cysts, or pockets, surrounded by scars in the pancreas, an organ that secretes digestive enzymes and insulin. Andersen found scars, along with cell damage and infection, in the lungs as well, and realized that the pancreas and lung damage were part of a single disease process, which she called cystic fibrosis of the pancreas. *Cystic* refers to the cysts she found, and *fibrosis* refers to the fibrous scar tissue that forms to replace damaged or infected cells. The name was later changed to simply cystic fibrosis.

A color-enhanced X-ray shows cystic fibrosis, a hereditary disease that causes certain glands to produce abnormal secretions of mucus in various organs.

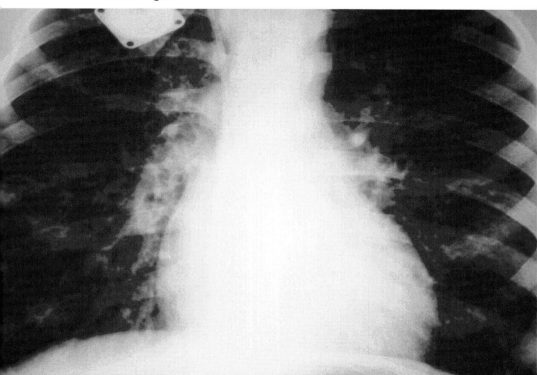

Dorothy Hansine Andersen

Dorothy Hansine Andersen was born on May 15, 1901, in Asheville, North Carolina. Her early life was difficult—her mother was an invalid and her father passed away when Dorothy was thirteen—and Dorothy overcame many obstacles then and throughout her life. She put herself through school and graduated from Mount Holyoke College, then earned her medical degree from Johns Hopkins University in 1926.

She completed her training as a surgical intern at Strong Memorial Hospital in Rochester, New York, but was turned down for further surgical training because of her gender. In an era when there were few female doctors, she instead took a position as a teacher and pathologist at Columbia University.

Part of her job as a pathologist involved performing autopsies to determine the cause of patient deaths, and during one child's autopsy she noticed scars in the pancreas. She began researching similar cases and discovered that many children had similar scars, along with inflammation and blockages in the lungs. She realized these problems were part of a single disease she named cystic fibrosis of the pancreas in 1938.

Andersen received many awards for her work in medicine, as well as for standing up for women's rights. Colleagues described her as a rugged individualist who enjoyed fixing her own home, including putting up a new roof. According to the National Women's Hall of Fame, "Throughout her career she was deeply committed to professional equality and refused to pattern her life according to conventional ideas of what was suitable for women." Andersen died of lung cancer in 1963.

National Women's Hall of Fame. "Dorothy H. Andersen." www.greatwomen.org /women-of-the-hall/search-the-hall-results/details/2/177-Andersen.

In the 1940s other doctors began uncovering further details about CF. Many found that affected children had thick, sticky mucus clogging the ducts (channels) in the lungs, pancreas, liver, sweat glands, and reproductive glands. Because of this finding, Sydney Farber of Children's Hospital in Boston began referring to the disorder as mucoviscidosis, meaning "thick mucus," but this name did not endure.

In 1948 and 1952 severe heat waves in New York City led to further clues about the characteristics of CF. Many babies and children with CF became dehydrated and were admitted to area hospitals. Paul di Sant'Agnese and his colleagues at Columbia University discovered that the dehydration resulted from the children losing abnormally large amounts of sodium and chloride (the elements in salt) in their sweat. Prior to this time, experts did not know why the skin of people with CF tasted salty, and the discovery was a major breakthrough. An article called "The History of Cystic Fibrosis" notes, "Undoubtedly the major advance during the Fifties was the recognition of the increased salt content of the sweat in people with CF by Paul di Sant'Agnese."[6] This finding was important because it led to an understanding of how and why the various symptoms of CF are related.

Following this advance, doctors discovered that abnormalities in the salt content of cells called epithelial cells that line the lungs, pancreas, liver, sweat glands, and reproductive glands are responsible for the mucus blockages that characterize the disease. Epithelial cells produce mucus, and when too much salt is released, the mucus becomes thick and sticky. Doctors also discovered that the symptoms related to mucus blockages depend on the function of each affected organ or gland.

The Lungs

The lungs are the most prominent part of the respiratory, or pulmonary, system that allows people to breathe. The respiratory system's main function is to bring life-giving oxygen into the body and to expel carbon dioxide waste products. Air is inhaled through the nose or mouth, then goes through the windpipe (trachea) into several layers of branching tubes called bronchial tubes, or bronchi, that lead into the lungs.

When air reaches the lungs, it goes into tiny sacs called alveoli. Alveoli act like tiny balloons that inflate and deflate with each breath. The lungs also consist of a network of air tubes and blood vessels. When air inflates the alveoli, oxygen from the air passes through the alveoli cell walls and enters the tiny blood vessels, or capillaries, that surround the alveoli. The oxygen then travels in red blood cells throughout the body. Without oxygen, body tissues die.

Red blood cells also carry waste products in the form of carbon dioxide from tissues back to the lungs, where the alveoli take in the carbon dioxide and release it into the bronchi. From there it is exhaled through the nose or mouth.

In addition to taking in air and releasing carbon dioxide, bronchi also secrete mucus. As the National Institutes of Health explains, "When we breathe, mucus is there to keep us protected, trapping particles and bacteria and moving these away from the lungs."[7] Mucus also keeps the lungs moist. The mucus-producing epithelial cells, along with tiny hairs called cilia, line the bronchial walls. Cilia push trapped bacteria and other harmful substances upward so they can be expelled with a sneeze or cough.

CF and the Respiratory System

When someone has CF, cilia cannot clear the overly thick, sticky mucus and bacteria from the lungs and bronchi. This can result in infections, breathing difficulties, and eventual respiratory failure. When the lungs do not work properly, blood oxygen levels fall too low and carbon dioxide levels become too high, which is fatal if not reversed. Mucus blockages can also lead to heart disease and heart failure because the heart is strained by trying to pump more blood to bring oxygen throughout the body.

Besides respiratory failure, which is the most common fatal complication of CF, other respiratory problems that result from excessive mucus buildup frequently occur in CF patients. One such problem is asthma, which involves tightened bronchial muscles and inflamed airways. Another complication, sinusitis, involves infection, irritation, and blockages in the sinus cavities behind the nose, eyes, and forehead, and can be extremely painful. Nose polyps (small growths in the nose) can also result from and worsen breathing problems.

Several other serious respiratory complications are atelectasis, where a completely blocked airway leaves part of the lung with no air; emphysema, which occurs when air becomes trapped in alveoli; pneumothorax, a collapsed lung, which results from burst alveoli; chronic obstructive pulmonary disease, in which mucus blocks and inflames the bronchi, leading

A microscopic view of a mucus-producing cell is seen here. The mucus-producing cells of cystic fibrosis sufferers produce an abnormal level of sticky mucus that makes it hard for them to breathe.

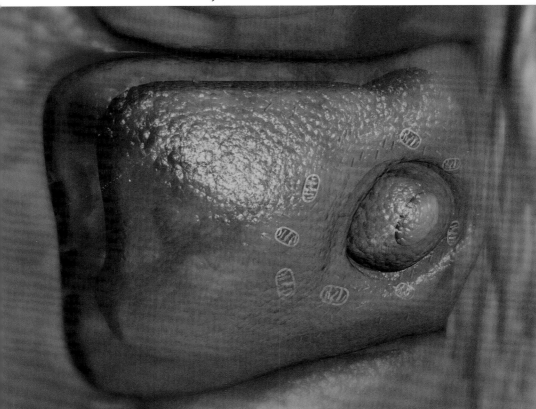

to coughing and wheezing; and bronchiectasis, a condition in which damaged airways become flabby and scarred.

All of these problems can contribute to respiratory failure, along with the frequent bronchial and lung infections that plague people with CF. Infections are in fact responsible for 95 percent of cases of fatal respiratory failure in people with the disease. When these infections lodge in the bronchi, they are known as bronchitis. When they settle in the lungs, they are called pneumonia. Infections that are not eradicated quickly further aggravate breathing difficulties and permanently inflame and damage epithelial cells. In response to these infections, the immune system sends in white blood cells to fight the organisms that cause the infection. When these white blood cells die, their DNA is released into the surrounding mucus, making it even stickier. The body also produces more mucus in an attempt to flush out the microorganisms that cause infections, and this leads to a vicious cycle of infection, inflammation, and worsening breathing difficulties. Ongoing lung infections can also produce potentially fatal lung bleeds that result in a patient coughing up blood. These lung bleeds occur when infections inflame and enlarge blood vessels, which then burst.

Bacteria, viruses, and fungi are all microorganisms that can cause respiratory infections. The most commonly seen infections in people with CF are from *Staphylococcus aureus*, *Pseudomonas aeruginosa*, and *Burkholderia cepacia* bacteria. All are very difficult to eradicate. Many patients also develop an allergy to a fungus called aspergillus, which lives in hay, rotting compost, and old buildings. If an allergic person inhales this fungus, wheezing and more severe breathing difficulties can result.

Since people with CF are so susceptible to serious lung infections, doctors recommend that they try to avoid germs as much as possible. According to the CFF:

> Although germs are everywhere and cannot be avoided, one of the best ways to keep from catching or spreading germs is through effective hand-washing, whether with

soap and water or alcohol-based hand gels. Everyone with CF should avoid unnecessary contact with people who have a cold or any other contagious illness, and should cough and sneeze into a tissue.[8]

Although CF itself is not contagious, the infections patients develop are, and preventing others from becoming infected is as important as the patient's avoiding infection sources.

The Digestive System

Besides the lungs, the other organ system most affected by CF is the digestive system, which brings food into the body, processes the food, and eliminates waste. Food goes through the mouth, down the throat, through the esophagus, and to the stomach, where it is partially digested. Then it goes to the small intestine, where digestion (the breakdown of proteins, fats, and carbohydrates into usable amino acids, fatty acids, and sugars respectively) is completed and usable nutrients are released into the bloodstream. Waste is passed to the colon, or large intestine, to be excreted.

The main effects of CF on the digestive system are in the final phases of digestion in the small intestine. This organ secretes some digestive enzymes of its own and also receives enzymes from the liver and pancreas. The liver releases bile salts into the small intestine through bile ducts; bile helps digest fats. Cells called acini in the pancreas produce the enzymes trypsin, chymotrypsin, and lipase, which digest proteins and fats. Acini send these enzymes into the intestine through pancreatic ducts.

In people with CF, epithelial cells lining the liver and pancreas produce large amounts of thick, sticky mucus that blocks the flow of these enzymes. When these chemicals sit in the pancreas, in particular, they essentially start digesting the pancreas itself, leading to the characteristic cysts and scar tissue. Eventually, the pancreas can become so damaged that other pancreatic cells, known as islet or beta cells, which produce insulin, are also destroyed. The subsequent lack of normal insulin production can lead to diabetes.

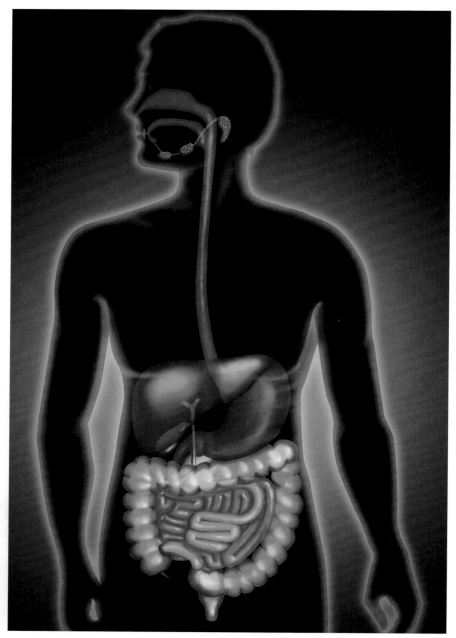

The human digestive system's principal organs include the stomach, liver, pancreas, and intestines. People with cystic fibrosis produce large amounts of mucus that inhibits the function of their digestive systems.

Insulin allows cells throughout the body to take in glucose, the body's main source of energy, from the bloodstream. Without insulin, diabetes occurs. In diabetes, blood sugar rises to dangerous levels, resulting in serious complications in the eyes, kidneys, nerves, and circulatory system and in coma and death if untreated. The type of diabetes related to CF is called cystic fibrosis–related diabetes (CFRD). It differs from the more common forms, known as type 1 and type 2 diabetes. Type 1 is an autoimmune disease in which the immune system destroys beta cells. Type 2 usually results from being overweight—the beta cells do produce insulin, but body cells become resistant to it or the beta cells do not produce enough insulin. People with CFRD have features in common with both type 1 and type 2. With CFRD beta cells often do not make enough insulin because of scarring in the pancreas, and many affected people also develop insulin resistance, which prevents their bodies from using insulin correctly.

More than 25 percent of adults with CF have CFRD. Thus, all CF patients are given blood tests for diabetes at least yearly.

Nutritional Problems

In addition to damaging the pancreas, when pancreatic enzymes cannot get to the small intestine, proteins and fats are not completely digested and are expelled as waste. This can lead to malnourishment, even when the individual consumes an adequate amount of food. Since the body lacks essential nutrients, normal growth may not occur, and overall weakness and an inability to fight infections may result.

The fact that people with CF excrete more waste than normal also results in bulky, fatty, extremely foul-smelling stools and sometimes in intestinal blockages. When such blockages occur before birth, this is known as meconium ileus. In some cases a blockage causes the intestine to burst before birth, and this can be fatal. If a baby is born with meconium ileus, he or she will vomit and can die unless the blockage is removed.

Another result of a lack of pancreatic enzymes can be osteoporosis (thin, brittle bones). Usually, osteoporosis occurs in older people, but in those with CF, insufficient absorption of

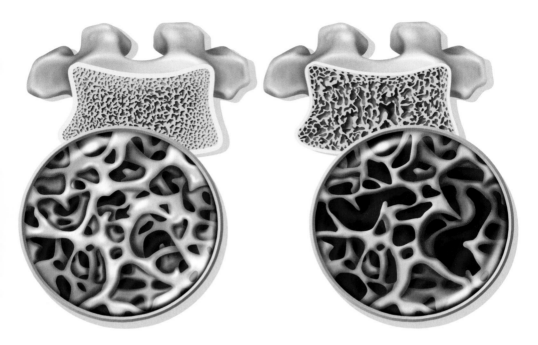

Poor digestion resulting from cystic fibrosis can lead to nutritional deficiencies that, in turn, can cause diseases such as osteoporosis, a weakening of the bones. This illustration shows a normal vertebra, left, and one affected by osteoporosis.

calcium and vitamin D means it often happens much sooner. Daniel Markovich, author of *Cystic Fibrosis Handbook for Patient and Family*, explains, "Osteoporosis has come to be recognized as a significant problem for the adolescent and adult with CF—in fact, it appears to be present in virtually all who survive to early adulthood."[9] Bone thickness, or density, can be assessed with imaging tests called bone density tests. Since low bone density and osteoporosis can lead to frequent bone breaks and much pain, doctors recommend that all CF patients receive frequent bone density tests.

Not all people with CF experience the nutritional deficiencies that lead to serious complications like osteoporosis and malnutrition, however. In some, enough pancreatic enzymes are produced and get through to the small intestine to make digestion fairly normal. These individuals are known as pancreatic sufficient. However, about 85 percent of CF patients are pancreatic insufficient. Doctors can assess pancreatic sufficiency by testing patients' stools for fat content and for an enzyme called elastase. Abnormally low amounts of elastase and abnormally high amounts of fat mean someone is pancreatic insufficient.

Although most people with CF suffer from pancreatic insufficiency, far fewer experience complications from liver enzymes being blocked by mucus. About 40 percent of children with CF show evidence of liver abnormalities (assessed with blood tests called liver function tests) by age ten. However, less than 5 percent develop liver damage that is severe enough to lead to liver failure. Unlike pancreatic mucus blockages, which can lead to both tissue destruction and malnutrition, blockages of bile ducts in the liver do not affect digestion or absorption of nutrients to a significant degree. Liver blockages can, however, result in scarring called cirrhosis, and this in turn can impede the ability of the liver to perform its vital functions of clearing toxins from the blood and producing proteins such as those needed for blood clotting. Cirrhosis can also block the flow of blood in the liver, and this can increase pressure in the main vein leading to the liver. This increased pressure can induce fluid buildup or bleeding in the abdomen. Since most people with liver problems like these do not experience any symptoms until the damage is extensive, doctors routinely monitor CF patients' liver function in an attempt to detect abnormalities before they become life threatening.

Exocrine Glands and CF

Along with affecting the respiratory and digestive systems, CF also impacts exocrine glands—the sweat and reproductive glands that secrete chemicals through ducts rather than directly into the bloodstream through cell walls, like endocrine glands do. Sweat glands primarily help regulate body temperature and get rid of some waste products. Sweat contains mostly sodium and chloride, plus some calcium and potassium. Most people produce between 1 pint (473ml) and 0.5 gallons (1.9L) of sweat per day. People have more than 2 million coiled sweat glands in the skin's outermost layer, the epidermis. Each sweat gland releases sweat through a sweat duct, and each coiled sweat gland would measure over 4 feet (1.2m) long if it were uncoiled. The human body contains about 6 miles (9.7km) of sweat ducts.

Sweat normally moves from the base of the sweat gland through the duct to the skin's surface. Chloride channels (gates) line these ducts and normally reabsorb chloride after sweat leaves the body. These channels become blocked in CF, and chloride gets left on the skin's surface. This results in more sodium ions (charged atoms), which are attracted to chloride ions, leaving the sweat glands, and the excess sodium and chloride

A patient has a sweat test for cystic fibrosis. People with CF cannot reabsorb the chloride in their sweat and it gets left on the skin's surface, making the skin saltier than normal.

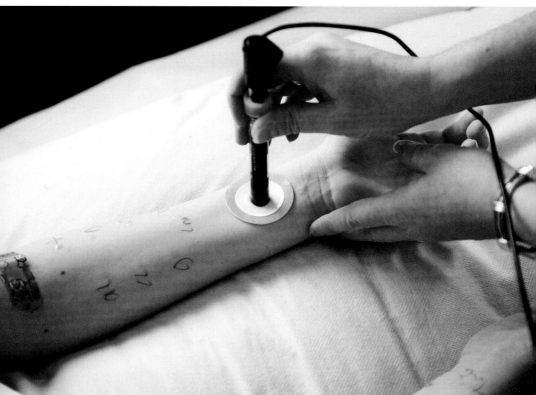

loss results in salty skin. This loss of salt places patients at high risk of dehydration after exercise or in hot weather.

The other affected exocrine glands—the reproductive glands—consist of the testicles in men and the ovaries in women. Testicles produce sperm and deliver it to the penis via a tube called the vas deferens. Ovaries produce eggs that travel through the fallopian tubes to the cervix at the base of the uterus. These processes begin at puberty when sex hormones become active.

Males and females with CF usually produce sex hormones and thus begin to mature sexually, but thick mucus blocks the vas deferens in men and often causes this tube to degenerate. In women mucus blocks the cervix, preventing eggs from being fertilized. Thus, most people with CF are infertile, or unable to produce children. Some women are able to conceive, but often doctors advise against this because pregnancy can worsen CF complications.

Diagnosing CF

Sex-related symptoms of CF are not life threatening, and, obviously, they do not become apparent until a patient reaches adolescence. Symptoms related to the sweat glands, lungs, and digestive system, on the other hand, are usually apparent at birth or shortly thereafter, and over 70 percent of patients are diagnosed by age two. Some people with mild symptoms, however, are not diagnosed until adolescence or adulthood, since mild symptoms can resemble those of other disorders and make an accurate diagnosis challenging. In addition, people with mild symptoms are usually pancreatic sufficient, which can further mask the fact that they actually have CF. According to an article in the journal *Current Opinion in Pulmonary Medicine*, "Often these patients have previously received diagnoses of asthma, chronic bronchitis, or emphysema. Pancreatic insufficiency is much less common in the adult receiving the diagnosis, but pancreatitis [severe inflammation of the pancreas] occurs with greater frequency."[10]

Today more and more cases of CF, even milder cases, are being diagnosed at birth because newborns in the United States

Potential Benefits and Harms of Newborn Screening for Cystic Fibrosis (CF)

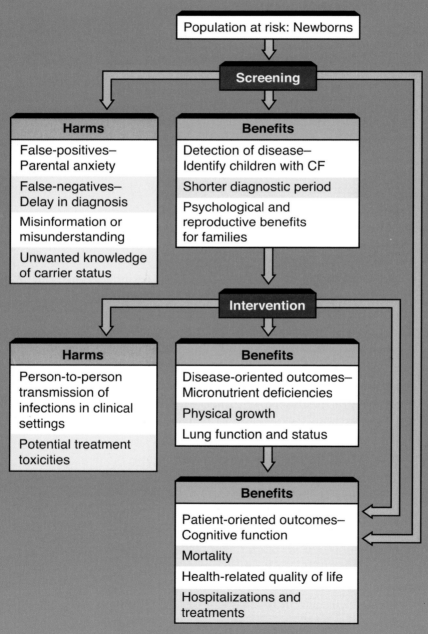

Population at risk: Newborns

Screening

Harms
- False-positives–Parental anxiety
- False-negatives–Delay in diagnosis
- Misinformation or misunderstanding
- Unwanted knowledge of carrier status

Benefits
- Detection of disease–Identify children with CF
- Shorter diagnostic period
- Psychological and reproductive benefits for families

Intervention

Harms
- Person-to-person transmission of infections in clinical settings
- Potential treatment toxicities

Benefits
- Disease-oriented outcomes–Micronutrient deficiencies
- Physical growth
- Lung function and status

Benefits
- Patient-oriented outcomes–Cognitive function
- Mortality
- Health-related quality of life
- Hospitalizations and treatments

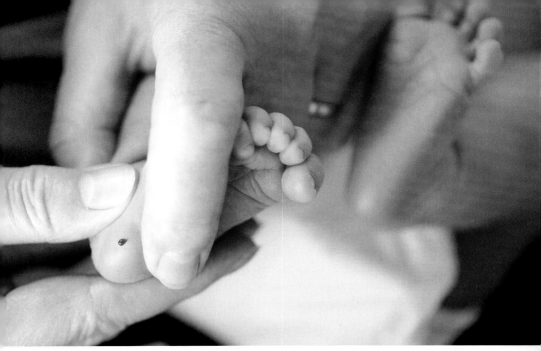

More CF cases are being diagnosed at birth because newborns are now routinely screened for the disease with a heel-prick blood test (shown) right after birth.

and in several other countries are now routinely screened for the disease with a heel-prick blood test. This test detects levels of an enzyme called immunoreactive trypsin. If levels of this enzyme are elevated, doctors confirm the diagnosis of CF with a sweat test. In places where newborns are not screened routinely, infants, children, or adults who show symptoms of recurrent lung infections; bulky, fatty stools; or failure to gain weight when plenty of food is being ingested will receive a sweat test after symptoms appear.

With a sweat test, technicians place two pads containing a chemical called pilocarpine on the forearm and force the chemical into the skin with a mild electric current. The pads are removed, and the pilocarpine causes sweat to be released. The sweat is collected for about thirty minutes with a special sweat-collecting disc containing a tube. Technicians then analyze the sweat for chloride. If the concentration of chloride is greater than sixty millimoles per liter, an individual receives a diagnosis of CF.

Doctors can also confirm a CF diagnosis by conducting genetic tests for gene mutations associated with the disease, but as the authors of the book *The Facts: Cystic Fibrosis* explain, "The usual laboratory tests will only detect about 30 of the most common genetic mutations so will make diagnosis in only about 75 per cent of cases. As over 1500 mutations causing cystic fibrosis have been identified it is possible for the usual laboratory test to miss a rare mutation. For this reason the sweat test is still used as the gold standard."[11]

Indeed, the nongenetic diagnostic tests for CF were developed many years before the genetic causes of the disease were identified, and these tests have proven to be very reliable. The discovery of the underlying causes, however, gave doctors an additional diagnostic tool and improved the understanding of CF, which has paved the way for improved treatments.

CHAPTER TWO

What Causes Cystic Fibrosis?

Although physicians learned a great deal about the symptoms and diagnosis of CF in the 1940s and 1950s, no one understood the causes of the disease until the late 1980s. Many doctors had proposed that certain dietary deficiencies, such as a vitamin A deficiency, caused CF, but by the 1940s doctors realized that nutritional deficiencies resulted from, rather than caused, the disease. Dorothy Andersen was among the first to hypothesize a genetic cause, based on the fact that CF seemed to run in families, but no one proved this theory until 1989.

Progress toward proving a genetic cause began in the 1980s with advances in understanding the cellular changes that underlie CF. Once scientists understood these cellular changes, they realized that genes that control these processes had to be responsible for the changes. Paul M. Quinton at the University of California–Riverside first made headway in this regard when he discovered that the epithelial cells that line sweat glands in people with CF do not reabsorb negatively charged chloride ions and that this leads positively charged sodium ions to follow these chloride ions to the skin's surface.

Also in the 1980s, researchers Michael Knowles and Richard Boucher of the University of North Carolina–Chapel Hill discovered that similar defects exist in epithelial cells in the lungs of CF patients. They found that, as with sweat gland epithelial

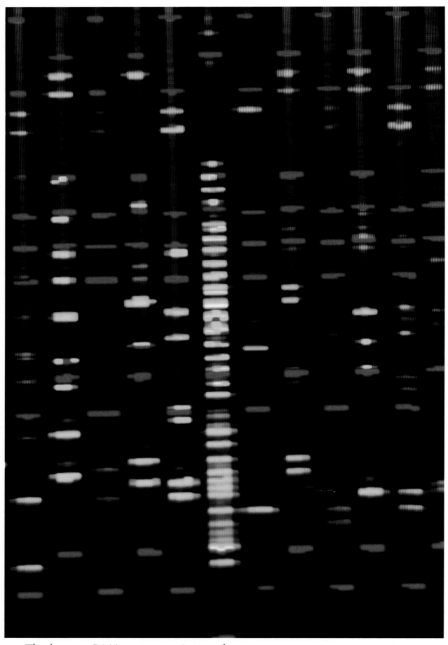

The human DNA sequence is seen here on a computer screen.
Medical researchers in the 1980s proved that cystic fibrosis was
caused by a genetic mutation.

cells, blocked chloride channels in lung epithelial cells prevented chloride ion movement. Too much salt and not enough water in these mucus-producing cells in turn led to thick, sticky mucus buildup in the lungs. Quinton later wrote in a *Physiological Reviews* article that Knowles and Boucher's discovery indicated that an identical process was causing symptoms of CF in different organs, and that this underlying process involved defects in chloride ion movement, rather than resulting from mucus buildup itself: "This finding in 1981 provided the first physiological link between the lung, the pancreas, and the sweat gland. The common link was not mucus, but electrolytes [electrically charged chemicals]."[12]

Once scientists understood that defects in chloride ion movement underlie the diverse symptoms of CF, they realized that defects in genes that encode instructions for chloride movement across cell membranes were most likely to blame for these cellular abnormalities. Thus, they began searching for the responsible genes.

Genes and Gene Mutations

Genes are the parts of deoxyribonucleic acid (DNA) molecules that pass hereditary information from parents to their offspring. They reside on wormlike bodies called chromosomes in the center, or nucleus, of each cell. The sequence of genes on each chromosome provides a set of instructions telling the cell how to grow and operate. A baby is born with two sets of genetic instructions; one from the father and one from the mother. Humans have forty-six chromosomes in each cell. Twenty-three come from the father and twenty-three from the mother. The genes on each chromosome also come in pairs, with one copy from each parent.

Damage to a gene or chromosome is called a mutation. Mutations can involve an entire chromosome, one or more genes, or one or more of the chemical base pairs called nucleotides that make up DNA. DNA molecules contain two strands of nucleotides, which include the bases adenine, thymine, guanine, and cytosine. The strands are twisted into a ladder-like double helix structure that always pairs adenine with thymine and guanine with cytosine. The sequence of nucleotides determines the instructions coded and issued by a particular gene. Damage to or absence of even one nucleotide in a sequence of thousands can completely disrupt the genetic instructions.

Any mutation can be passed to a baby if it happens to be part of the set of chromosomes and genes transmitted from either parent, and these mutations can lead to malfunctions that produce certain diseases. Though scientists suspected that one or more gene mutations that led to faulty instructions being issued for chloride ion movement in cells was probably responsible for CF, finding the faulty gene was not an easy task.

Searching for Genes

Finding a gene or gene mutation is difficult, even with high-tech equipment that allows scientists to see and manipulate these submicroscopic structures. In the 1980s it was even more difficult than it is today. Researchers still use electron microscopes and chemicals that separate DNA strands to search for genes like they did in the 1980s, but today they also have more efficient techniques and computer programs available for analyzing data.

Humans have a total of twenty thousand to twenty-five thousand genes, so locating a particular gene or mutation and determining its function can be time consuming. Some mutations are relatively easy to spot because they involve an easily seen break in an entire chromosome. But scientists searching for the CF gene found that any mutations did not include chromosome breaks. In fact, it turned out that they involved only one or more misplaced nucleotides, which are very difficult to detect.

Many scientists tried to locate the CF gene. Lap-Chee Tsui and John Riordan and their colleagues at the Toronto Hospital for Sick Children in Canada were part of one dedicated team that began their search in 1982 using a technique called linkage analysis. This method is based on the finding that genes lying close together on a chromosome are inherited as a unit. The scientists looked for sequences of DNA known as genetic markers that appeared regularly in families and individuals known to have CF. Identifying these sequences would allow researchers to link these sequences to the disease.

Lap-Chee Tsui

Lap-Chee Tsui (pronounced Choy) was born in Shanghai, China, on December 21, 1950, and grew up in Tai Koon Yu, Hong Kong. As a boy he dreamed of becoming an architect but went on to receive degrees in biology from the Chinese University of Hong Kong, followed by a PhD in biology from the University of Pittsburgh in 1979.

Tsui went to work at Oak Ridge National Laboratory in Tennessee, where he developed an interest and specialty in genetics. In 1981 he moved to Canada to conduct genetic research and teach at the Hospital for Sick Children and the University of Toronto. His genetic research centered on searching for the gene that causes CF, and in 1989 he became internationally known when he and his colleagues identified the *CFTR* gene.

He later made many contributions to decoding the human genome (the complete set of human DNA), and in 2002 he moved back to Hong Kong to become vice chancellor of the University of Hong Kong. Over the years he has received many awards for his research and breakthroughs in the field of genetics, but finding the *CFTR* gene remains his most famous achievement.

Lap-Chee Tsui, left, headed a team that located genetic markers for CF in 1985.

In 1985 Tsui and scientists from two other laboratories published their findings that genetic markers for CF appeared on
chromosome seven. This was an important step, explains the
Howard Hughes Medical Institute (HHMI), because "up to that
point, looking for the CF gene had been much like trying to
find a particular house without even knowing what continent
it was on. Now researchers could narrow their search to an
area equivalent to a particular country."[13]

The next step involved further study of DNA from people
with and without CF to narrow down the area of chromosome
seven where the gene was located. But Tsui realized that analyzing many DNA sections would take about eighteen years, so
he collaborated with Francis Collins of the University of Michi-
gan to pioneer a new method of examining chromosomes for
additional genetic markers.

Collins had recently developed a method of analyzing one
hundred thousand to two hundred thousand DNA molecules at
a time. He called the new technique "jumping," since it allowed
scientists to jump, rather than walk along a chromosome
searching for genes. The HHMI explains, "'Walking' toward the
CF gene was too slow. For geneticists, walking along a chromosome means using partly overlapping DNA fragments to
move toward the target gene, one step at a time, checking each
fragment to see whether it is inherited with the disease. It is an
arduous task. The path is strewn with repetitive sequences of
DNA or other stretches difficult to cross."[14]

To jump, scientists cut up a DNA strand with chemicals
called restriction enzymes. They then label one end of the
sliced-up DNA piece and allow it to curl into a circle that puts
the labeled end next to a section of DNA that was previously
hundreds or thousands of base chemicals away. Going from
one labeled end to another and skipping over sequences that
are irrelevant to the disease being studied allows the researchers to quickly search for genetic markers. The HHMI
states that "jumping is five to ten times faster than walking. It
allows researchers to cover 100,000 to 200,000 DNA bases at
one time and simply leap over areas that might otherwise be
difficult to cross."[15] Researchers today have newer techniques

that would have made this task a lot easier, but until the human genome (entire DNA blueprint) was decoded in 2003, jumping was state-of-the-art.

Jumping allowed Tsui to find additional genetic markers on chromosome seven and eventually to locate the CF gene using these markers. He and his colleagues then found a mutation in the sweat gland, pancreas, and lung cells of 70 percent of people with CF. This mutation was absent in people without CF, indicating that it caused the disease. The discovery created a great deal of excitement among researchers and patients when Tsui reported it in 1989. Knowing which gene caused CF could be useful in developing new treatments and even a cure.

Characteristics of the CF Gene

Tsui's finding was hailed as a major achievement not only because it brought scientists closer to developing a cure for CF, but also because it helped in diagnosis, particularly in embryos. Doctors could now extract DNA from an embryo or fetus and inform the parents whether their baby would be born with this genetic defect. It also allowed adults who do not have CF but have a family history of the disease to be tested to see whether they carry the mutation. This can help them decide whether they wish to reproduce and risk passing the mutation on to their children.

Further research determined just how parents transmit the CF gene. Genes are either dominant or recessive. Dominant genes dominate, or override, recessive genes. If a child inherits a dominant gene for a particular trait from the mother and a recessive gene for the same trait from the father, the dominant trait will prevail. For instance, the gene for brown eyes is dominant and for blue eyes recessive, so a baby who inherits one brown-eyed gene and one blue-eyed gene will have brown eyes. Only if both parents supply a recessive gene will their offspring show that trait.

The CF gene is recessive. Thus, a child who develops CF inherits two defective copies of the gene—one from each parent. People who inherit only one copy do not get the disease but are called carriers because they carry the defective gene and

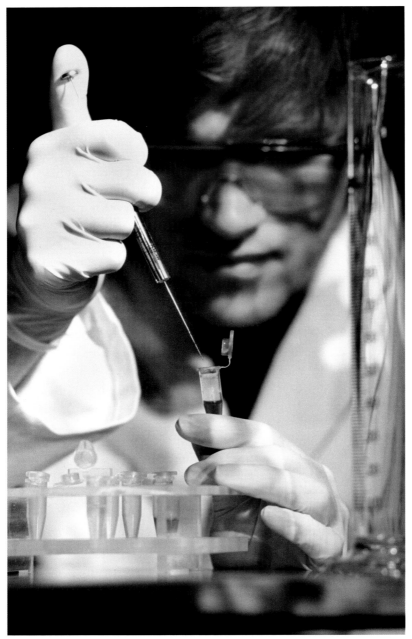

A biologist extracts DNA from a sample. Doctors can now extract DNA from a fetus and inform the parents whether their baby will be at risk for cystic fibrosis.

can pass it on to their children. Carriers have a 50 percent chance of transmitting the defective gene. This means that a child of two CF carriers has a 25 percent chance of getting CF and a 50 percent chance of being a carrier. Experts estimate that there are about 10 million CF carriers in the United States today.

If one parent has CF and the other parent is a carrier, a child has a 50 percent chance of getting the disease. These odds convince most such couples not to reproduce. However, many couples who are both carriers are unaware of this fact and find out only after they produce a child with CF. As the author of *Cystic Fibrosis Handbook for Patient and Family* explains:

> The number of undetected carriers of an abnormal CF gene may be as high as 3 percent of the population, so it's not unlikely for two such affected individuals to meet, marry and have children—and one child in four will have CF. For the foreseeable future we'll continue to see CF children being born without prior warning because the parents appear unaffected. At present, we don't screen for carriers in the general population, because the tests are expensive and technically difficult to perform in large numbers. If simple, inexpensive screening tests become available, earlier detection of people at risk for having a CF child may be possible. For now, though, genetic screening is only recommended to those with a strong history of CF in their immediate families.[16]

If both members of a couple have CF, it is very unlikely that they will be able to conceive a baby because of the disease's effect on the reproductive glands. If this did happen, however, the baby would be 100 percent certain to have CF.

How Does the CF Gene Work?

After identifying and characterizing the way the CF gene is transmitted, researchers went on to determine how mutations in the gene cause CF. Tsui's team found that the mutation that causes the disease in the majority of patients results from an absence of 3 of the gene's 250,000 nucleotides. The missing nucleotides lead to the loss of 1 amino acid (protein building block) out of 1,480 amino acids that make up the protein that the gene instructs cells to make. This tiny defect is sufficient to cause the disruptions in chloride movement that underlie CF. A defective protein closes chloride channels in the cell membrane, and this makes the cells unable to adjust the consistency of the mucus they secrete.

Because mutated CF genes issue faulty instructions for manufacturing the protein that regulates chloride movement across epithelial cell membranes, scientists named the gene the cystic fibrosis transmembrane conductance regulator (*CFTR*) gene and the related protein the CFTR protein. To avoid confusing the gene and protein, the name of the gene is usually italicized in the scientific literature and the name of the protein is not.

Later studies showed that many different *CFTR* gene mutations can lead to the production of a defective CFTR protein. To date, scientists have identified over fifteen hundred such mutations. Most of these mutations occur rarely; some are confined to people in only one of several families. People with CF can have one or more of these mutations, but the end result of all is the same—the disruption of chloride transport. However, the mechanism of action of each mutation differs slightly. Scientists have placed these mutations into five major categories that each affect the CFTR protein somewhat differently.

Mutations in the first category cause cells to produce an abnormal CFTR protein that lacks the amino acid phenylalanine. The most common mutation in this category, and incidentally, the most common CF mutation, is known as deltaF508. DeltaF508 affects 70 percent to 80 percent of CF patients. The *F* in the name stands for phenylalanine, and the *508* indicates that phenylalanine is missing from position number 508 in the sequence of 1,480 amino acids that make up the CFTR protein. The missing amino acid prevents this protein from folding and entering cell membranes normally. This in turn causes the chloride channel malfunction.

Mutations in the second major category keep the CFTR protein from being produced at all. When this happens, there are no chloride channels through which chloride can move. In the

It All Started Fifty Thousand Years Ago

Once scientists identified the CF gene and found that many mutations in this gene can cause the disease, they traced the origins of the mutations using chromosome analysis. With this method, genetics experts measure the length of a stretch of DNA in which a mutation appears in a person with a particular genetic disease. This stretch of DNA is called a haplotype. The measurement allows scientists to calculate the approximate date when the mutation first appeared in humans. This is because haplotypes get shorter over time as more people's genes mingle in the world's growing population.

Chromosome analysis led researchers to conclude that the first CF gene mutations appeared about fifty thousand years ago in people in southeastern Europe and the Middle East. Each type of *CFTR* mutation can be traced to a single person in these areas and is thus known as a founder mutation. All people today who have these mutations share a common ancestor, or founder, in whom the particular mutation first appeared. Studying founder mutations allows scientists to identify groups of people who are at risk for certain diseases. It also lets them trace the history and migrations of people throughout the world.

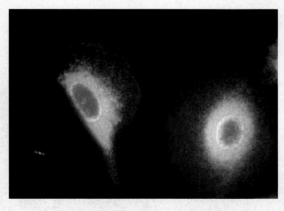

Researchers traced the genetic history of the CF-causing gene by studying DNA from specially cultured cells like these lung cells.

third category, cells produce the CFTR protein, but it is too small to function because the gene mutation directs the cell to stop producing the protein before it is complete.

The fourth mutation category occurs very rarely. Here, the abnormal *CFTR* gene allows a complete CFTR protein to move to the cell membrane but prevents chloride channels from opening up. In the fifth and final category, the mutated gene also allows a complete protein to be assembled, but a defective amino acid in the gene's DNA produces garbled messages that fail to instruct the cell to move chloride ions across the cell membrane. Chloride channels actually open up in this scenario, but close too quickly to allow the chemical to pass through.

Gene Mutations and Disease Severity

Many scientists have attempted to correlate each of these *CFTR* gene mutation categories with disease severity in different patients but have found conflicting results. In the case of category 5 mutations, most affected people have normal pancreas function but have the other typical CF symptoms. However, the severity of lung problems seems to vary even among patients with identical mutations. One study found that people with "class I or II mutations on both chromosomes have more rapid deterioration in lung function and lower survival rates,"[17] while other studies find no such correlation. In patients with the deltaF508 mutation, most have serious lung and digestive problems, but some do not, and scientists have concluded that environmental as well as other genetic factors may affect disease severity in those with CF. Biologists call this "genotype by environment," meaning that the particular genes a person has can be influenced by internal or external factors.

One such factor that CF experts believe may influence disease severity is the presence of modifier genes that do not directly cause CF, but which play a role in increasing or decreasing the intensity of symptoms in some patients. Researchers base this hypothesis on work by investigators at Johns Hopkins University who used genetic engineering to create laboratory mice with CF. Those mice that had certain modifier genes became less sick than other mice, and the researchers believe this may be because

A technician grafts genetically modified cells onto the organs of a mouse in order to study the effect of such cells on the severity of CF symptoms.

the modifier genes somehow activate alternative methods of moving chloride ions across cell membranes.

Scientists at the University of North Carolina–Chapel Hill are now pursuing related research on finding modifier genes in people with CF. These investigators are analyzing DNA from CF patients who have the same *CFTR* mutation (deltaF508) but who have varying degrees of disease severity. In hopes of narrowing the list of potential modifier genes, they are studying about two hundred genes they suspect may play a role in

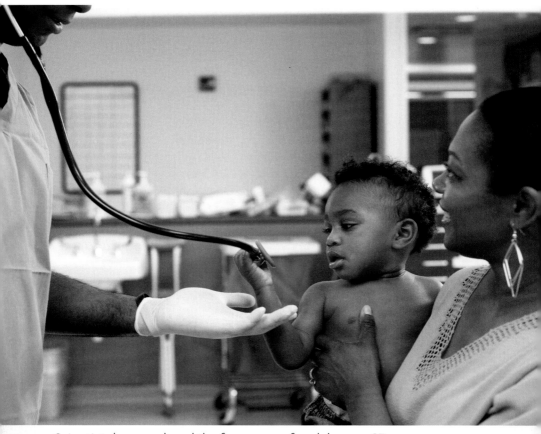

Scientists have analyzed the frequency of each known CF gene mutation in certain racial and ethnic groups. Forty-eight percent of African Americans with CF have the deltaF508 gene mutation.

modifying *CFTR* mutations to see which ones consistently appear in patients with mild or severe forms of the disease. The researchers will then attempt to determine exactly which modifier genes are responsible. "Identification of genetic modifiers (that may explain why 10 percent of CF patients died before the age of 10, $1/3$ before the age of 20 while 50 percent live over 32 years of age) should expand the therapeutic targets,"[18] the researchers write, explaining that once modifier genes are identified, treatments can focus on inserting or activating favorable modifier genes in patients who lack them.

CF Mutations and Patient Groups

In addition to studying the relationship between the various mutations and disease severity, scientists have also analyzed the frequency of each known mutation in certain racial and ethnic groups and have found distinct variations in certain groups and subgroups. Seventy percent of all Caucasians who have CF carry the deltaF508 mutation, while only 30 percent of the subset of Caucasian Ashkenazi Jews with CF have this mutation. Most of the remaining Ashkenazi Jews have a mutation called W1282X. Among African Americans with CF, about 48 percent have the deltaF508 mutation, while many others have mutations not seen in Caucasians with the disease. One common such mutation is 3120+1A->G. Being aware of which racial and ethnic groups most often carry certain *CFTR* muta-

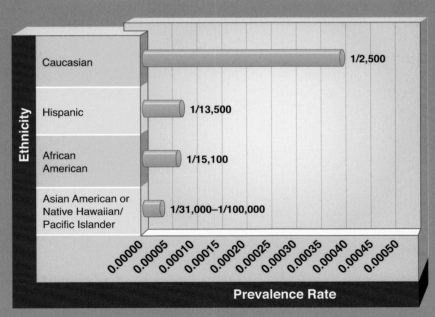

Taken from: Centers for Disease Control and Prevention. Cystic Fibrosis Clinical Validity, September 10, 2007.

tions helps doctors decide which genetic screening tests to administer to embryos and to possible carriers, since different screening tests look for different mutations.

Doctors enter data on mutations that appear in different groups or families into the Cystic Fibrosis Mutation Database maintained by the Cystic Fibrosis Center at the Hospital for Sick Children in Toronto, Canada. This database provides up-to-date information for doctors and scientists about screening recommendations and about newly discovered mutations that can cause CF. Experts use this data not only in screening and diagnosis, but also in research that seeks new and better CF treatments that target these genetic defects.

CHAPTER THREE

Cystic Fibrosis Treatment

Before doctors were aware of mucus blockages in the lungs and pancreases of people with CF, attempted treatments were ineffective because no one knew what the treatment targets should be. Even after the underlying problems were understood, effective treatments for lung infections did not come about until the introduction of penicillin in 1944 and other antibiotics shortly thereafter. Measures to improve patients' nutrition did not succeed until the use of pancreatic enzyme supplements became popular in the 1950s; prior to this time, doctors such as Dorothy Andersen prescribed special diets only.

Andersen advised "a low fat, high protein diet with a liberal allowance of vegetables, fruits and sugar and a moderate restriction of starch,"[19] plus vitamin A and B supplements to address the vitamin deficiencies she believed contributed to the disease. Andersen also advised parents to keep children with CF away from other people to prevent lung infections. Several doctors in the 1940s also began recommending that patients sleep in mist tents, which concentrated vaporizer steam into a small area to help clear the lungs.

Special diets, mist tents, and isolation, however, rarely prolonged patients' lives by themselves. But modern treatment plans that incorporate daily enzyme supplements and

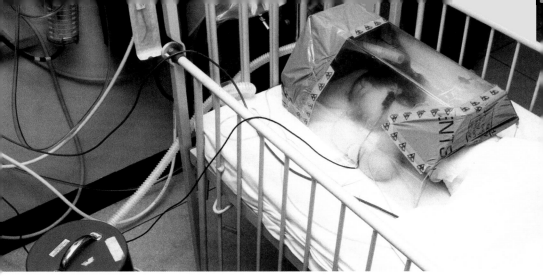

A child sleeps in a misting tent to help him breathe. Use of such tents was one of the earliest attempts to relieve CF symptoms.

mucus-clearing procedures, along with drugs to treat infections and complications as needed, have increased patients' life spans dramatically.

Monitoring and Treatment with a Team Approach

Given the complex, diverse symptoms involved, CF monitoring and treatment is usually administered by a team of doctors and other health-care professionals at a specialized CF center. Many studies have shown that patients who receive care at one of these centers do better overall than those who do not. Sometimes, however, patients do not live close enough to a CF center to go regularly or at all. In such cases their physicians often consult with specialists at a CF center, and if possible, the person travels to the center at least once a year.

Treatment teams usually consist of pediatricians for children and internal medicine specialists in digestion and breathing for adults, plus nurses who specialize in CF care, pharmacists to coordinate medications, physiotherapists who specialize in lung treatments, dieticians, and psychologists or social workers to address coping with the challenges faced by patients and families. Most patients are seen at a CF center for a checkup every three months to be weighed, measured, and given tests to assess lung function and the presence of infection. This way doctors can detect any emerging problems before they become serious, even if the person is feeling well, and appropriate treatment changes can be made.

One important monitoring test is a lung function test, which involves the patient blowing into a spirometer machine as fast and hard as possible. The machine measures forced vital capacity and forced expiratory volume to assess how well the person is inhaling and exhaling. A deterioration in lung function can reveal early signs of mucus plugs in the airways.

In other monitoring tests, doctors perform a throat swab or ask the patient to cough up sputum (mucus that has been coughed up) to test for infections. If the patient cannot cough anything up, the physician may have to put a tube called a bronchoscope down the throat and into the lungs to obtain mucus for testing. Once a year, blood tests, a chest X-ray, and a ventilation scan are performed to assess overall health, blood oxygen and carbon dioxide levels, and mucus plugs in the lungs.

A doctor monitors a patient's lung function test as the patient blows into a spirometer. The machine measures the amount and speed of air that is exhaled.

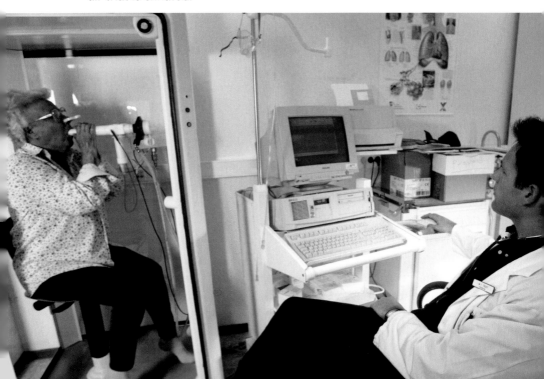

CF experts emphasize that the patient's and family's input about changes in the patient's condition, along with these regular monitoring tests, are important elements in any treatment plan. As physician Cori Daines states in a CFF article, "It is important that people with CF and their families consider themselves part of their care team. Rather than passively receiving treatment, people [should] take an active role in their treatment. When this happens, health care providers are better able to help people with CF achieve their individual goals."[20]

Ongoing Nutritional Treatments

The patient and family's active role in treatment is essential because CF therapy is an ongoing, everyday process with no vacations. A typical treatment program consists of following a high-calorie, high-fat diet; taking pancreatic enzyme pills; taking daily vitamin supplements; and performing daily inhalation and physiotherapy to clear mucus from the lungs.

The authors of *The Facts: Cystic Fibrosis* explain the reason for a high-calorie, high-fat diet:

> Most CF individuals are pancreatic insufficient. This means that they need supplementary enzymes to help digest their food. Supplementary enzymes are rarely as good as those produced naturally and so the recommendation is that someone with CF should aim to eat a diet which contains approximately 120 percent of the normal calorie requirements for a person of the same sex, weight, and age but who does not have cystic fibrosis. The aim should be for 30–40 percent of those calories to come from fat.[21]

Another reason for the extra calories is that people with CF use more energy than normal in day-to-day activities. This is because mucus blockages make the body work harder to do anything, including breathing. Gaining weight is therefore difficult for those with CF.

Patients must take pancreatic enzyme capsules with all meals and most snacks. A snack of only fruit or another sugar does not require enzymes because these enzymes only help digest proteins and fats. Most enzyme capsules contain granules

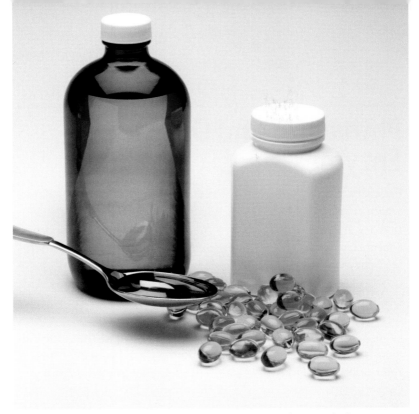

Cystic fibrosis patients need to supplement their diets with digestive enzymes and vitamins, especially the fat-soluble vitamins A, D, E, and K.

of the enzymes lipase, amylase, and protease that can be swallowed whole or opened and sprinkled on food.

Pancreatic enzymes can have side effects such as gas, bloating, diarrhea, and abdominal pain, so doctors are careful to prescribe doses that are high enough to help digestion but low enough to be less likely to cause side effects.

Besides enzyme supplements, CF patients also take vitamin supplements, since they have difficulty absorbing vitamins A, D, E, and K, which are absorbed with fat. All are needed to maintain healthy body processes. Vitamin A is especially important for eye health, vitamin D for bone health, vitamin E for nervous system health, and vitamin K for normal blood clotting.

Patients with osteoporosis in particular are advised to take vitamin D regularly, along with calcium supplements to help build and maintain bones. Regular weight-bearing exercise, such as walking or running, is also recommended for this purpose. Some

Phthalates and Digestive Enzymes

Recently, many people have been concerned about phthalates, which researchers have linked to various health problems in laboratory animals. Phthalates are chemicals used in plastics, drugs, soaps, cosmetics, and other products, including artificial pancreatic enzymes taken by CF patients. Phthalates are found in the coating around the small beads inside each enzyme capsule. This coating helps slow down the release of the enzymes so they stay effective longer.

In 2008 a team of Canadian researchers found that children who take pancreatic enzymes have more phthalates than normal in their urine. This led many parents to become concerned, but the Centers for Disease Control and Prevention (CDC) announced that no one has linked phthalates to specific health problems in humans, even though all people are exposed to these chemicals every day. The CDC also pointed out that many people without CF also excrete phthalates in their urine.

Based on these findings, the Cystic Fibrosis Foundation and the Food and Drug Administation have stated that "because the risk of malnutrition from not taking pancreatic enzymes is much greater than the potential risk related to phthalates, it is advised that people with CF continue taking their pancreatic enzymes as prescribed."

Cystic Fibrosis Foundation. "FAQs About Phthalates & Pancreatic Enzymes." www.cff.org/LivingWithCF/StayingHealthy/Diet/Phthalates.

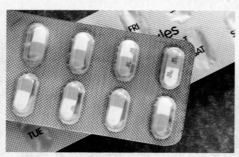

Phthalates are used in making plastics and some drugs. Their use in supplemental pancreatic enzymes has raised concern for CF patients.

patients with thinning bones are given drugs called bisphospho-
nates to build bone mass, but these drugs can have serious side
effects, and doctors say that taking vitamin supplements and ex-
ercising are much preferable, especially for children.

Even with vitamin and pancreatic enzyme supplements,
many patients still cannot digest and absorb enough nutrients
to grow properly and gain weight, and they may need supplemental feedings through a tube. One such method uses a naso-
gastric (NG) tube, which the patient inserts through the nose
into the stomach each night. A nutritional solution is passed
through the tube while the person sleeps. Inserting the tube is
unpleasant, and the feedings can lead to bloating and pain, so
many patients tend to resist using this method. Another type of
feeding tube, a gastrostomy, or G-, tube, is inserted by a doctor
through the abdomen, directly into the stomach or intestine,
and hooked up to a container that pumps in liquid food. Many
people find this permanently installed tube more tolerable than
the NG tube. Whichever method they use, though, patients say
the resulting weight and energy gains are well worth the incon-
venience.

Fifteen-year-old Kyle, for example, got used to inserting an
NG tube. He stated in a CFF article, "Tubefeeding has helped
me so much. I've gained over 25 pounds and grown four inches
in less than one year. Even my look has changed—I don't look
so scrawny anymore. . . . It's tough at first, but if you stick with
it, it can do so much for you."[22]

Veronica, on the other hand, found an NG tube intolerable,
so at age fourteen she allowed doctors to put in a G-tube and
was glad she did. She says:

> Once fully recovered from the surgery, I knew that having
> the G-tube would be a lot easier. No need to worry about
> putting the NG tube in every night and taking it out every
> morning and no more gagging. The G-tube would always
> be there and would be a constant reminder to do my feed-
> ings. The G-tube has completely changed my life for the
> better. It has helped in so many ways, not only gaining
> weight but gaining self-esteem and energy.[23]

A third type of tube feeding, parenteral nutrition, is generally used for short periods of time while a patient is hospital-
ized. With this method, doctors insert a tube into a major artery
in the chest and hook it up to a pump that sends liquid nutrition directly into the bloodstream.

Airway Clearance Techniques

Besides nutritional treatments, the other major part of daily CF
therapy involves twice-daily techniques of clearing mucus
from the lungs. This is known as physiotherapy or airway
clearance techniques (ACTs). According to the CFF, "ACTs
move mucus from small to large (more central) airways to be
coughed or huffed out."[24] Huffing is a breathing technique in
which the individual takes a medium-size breath, followed by a
fast breath through an open mouth to move mucus to a point
where it can be coughed out.

There are several types of ACTs. One technique, called percussion and drainage, is usually used on infants and small children since it requires another person. As children mature, they

A device called the Vest helps CF patients breathe by vibrating their
chest wall to loosen mucus.

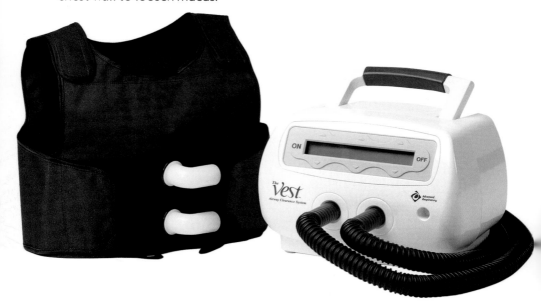

usually learn more independent ACTs. In percussion and drainage, the child is placed at various angles that allow gravity to drain mucus from each section of the lungs. An adult then claps on the skin over each targeted area with a cupped hand for about two minutes at a rate of three times per second. The child then huffs and coughs out freed mucus. Doctors say parents should perform this technique twice a day, even if the child is feeling well, to lengthen survival, but studies show that up to 40 percent of parents fail to administer it faithfully.

Another ACT is active cycle of breathing. With this technique, children older than five learn to breathe deeply in and out using the lower chest, followed by huffing and coughing. A similar technique called autogenic drainage is a bit more complicated and requires patients to learn to control their breathing at three different levels of lung expansion to loosen mucus.

Some patients use various devices to help clear the airways. One such device, the positive expiratory pressure (PEP) face mask, delivers air pressure that widens the airways while the person breathes out or huffs, making it easier to free up mucus. Another device, the flutter, or oscillating positive expiratory pressure device, contains a steel ball inside a pipe. The person breathes into the pipe, and this causes the ball to vibrate, which helps to clear the airways. The Acapella device is a combination PEP and flutter. It contains a plug and magnet, along with an adjustable valve, to create a vibration that forces out mucus.

A newer device called a therapy vest is becoming increasingly popular, but the cost of about twenty thousand dollars prevents many patients from obtaining this easy-to-use ACT. Most medical insurance plans will not fund the vest because less expensive alternatives are available. The vest is an air-filled jacket that vibrates the chest to loosen mucus. As with other ACTs, the patient then huffs and coughs to expel the mucus.

Several studies have analyzed which ACTs are most effective, but results are mixed. Some show therapy vests to be superior to percussion, while others find no reason to favor any technique or device. All studies do, however, indicate that combining physiotherapy with regular exercise is more effective than either is alone.

The authors of *The Facts: Cystic Fibrosis* explain, "Exercise has a very important role in keeping the lungs clear of mucus secretions. It encourages deep breathing and can be a very enjoyable part of treatment (and life) for many children. Bouncing games and trampolining are very useful physiotherapy aids. Exercise should be a supplement to and not a substitute for physiotherapy."[25] Doctors prescribe regular exercise such as running, bicycling, and team sports for patients in all age groups.

Other Lung Treatments and Compliance

Since many CF patients wheeze from airway inflammation, they require daily treatments with asthma inhalers or nebulizers in addition to daily ACTs. Inhalers contain medications such as albuterol to open up bronchial tubes. A nebulizer is a device that changes medication from a liquid to a mist form and delivers it into the lungs through a mask or mouthpiece. Most CF patients use nebulizers to deliver anti-inflammation medications, drugs that liquefy mucus, and antibiotics when needed for infections. One mucus-liquefying medication many people use is DNase, which breaks down long strands of DNA that make mucus in the lungs very sticky. Since DNase costs over one thousand dollars per month, some patients use concentrated saline (salt) solutions to achieve a similar result. DNase or saline are helpful in making ACTs more effective, and studies show they help prevent many lung infections and hospitalizations.

Doctors advise patients to perform nebulizer treatments twice a day along with ACTs. The combined treatments, along with setting up and cleaning equipment, usually take two to four hours per day, and many patients, especially adolescents, resent taking this much time away from other activities. Studies show that about 50 percent of adolescents with CF do less therapy than their doctors prescribe and about 30 percent do none at all. Many adults with CF and parents of children with the disease also do not stick with a treatment plan. Since compliance with therapy is considered critical for lengthening patients' lives, medical experts are concerned about these lapses. "The probable outcomes of poor adherence are exacerbations, weight loss and faster disease progression, which affects time away

Can Human Growth Hormone Help Children with CF?

Several studies have evaluated whether giving children and teens with CF injections of synthetic human growth hormone, known as somatropin, improves growth and lung function. Doctors know that even with pancreatic enzyme supplements, many patients fail to grow and gain weight normally. Some experts have proposed that somatropin might be helpful, but test results have not been promising. According to the Agency for Healthcare Research and Quality, part of the U.S. Department of Health and Human Services, "The available research cannot say if taking somatropin can help improve the quality or length of life for children or teens with CF." In addition, since somatropin increases the risk of diabetes and certain cancers, and since the injections cost tens of thousands of dollars per year, CF experts have concluded that this hormone should not be given to patients.

Agency for Healthcare Research and Quality, U.S. Department of Health and Human Services. *Human Growth Hormone for Children with Cystic Fibrosis: A Review of the Research for Parents and Caregivers*, March 2011. http://effective healthcare.ahrq.gov/index.cfm/search-for-guides-reviews-and-reports/?pageaction =displayproduct&productID=635.

from school and peers due to increased time spent in the hospital,"[26] write CF nurses at the Royal London Hospital.

Some patients who do not stick to a treatment plan do so for economic reasons. The annual cost of CF care is over forty thousand dollars per person, and even people who have medical insurance have high out-of-pocket costs in deductibles and copayments. Many skip doses of medications to make them last longer. The government provides financial assistance to low-income people in the form of Medicaid or sometimes certain types of Social Security benefits, but the costs for middle-class people can pose a burden on the family. In 2008 the Cystic Fibrosis Patient Assistance Foundation, a branch of the CFF, began helping insured patients and families with their expenses.

Lung Infections

Even patients who consistently do their ACT and other therapies still have mucus in their lungs, and sometimes it becomes or stays infected. Many doctors used to prescribe antibiotics to people even if they did not have an infection to prevent these infections, but most do not do this today because it leads to antibiotic-resistant bacteria. However, many patients have chronic lung infections, and in such cases ongoing treatment with various antibiotics may be necessary, even for years on end. Patients who have a cold or other illness caused by a virus (for which antibiotics are ineffective) are also given antibiotics, since having a cold makes it more likely that bacteria that normally live in the throat will enter and infect the lungs.

Some lung infections respond to treatment with oral antibiotics, but most are more easily eradicated or controlled with inhaled or intravenous drugs. Commonly used antibiotics are colomycin and tobramycin. Intravenous antibiotics can be administered in a hospital or at home using a portable chest catheter (permanently installed reservoir and tubes linked to veins under the skin) hooked up to IV bags. All antibiotics can have side effects such as stomach upsets and liver or kidney damage.

One type of bacteria, *Pseudomonas aeruginosa,* is particularly difficult to eradicate, and 60 percent to 80 percent of CF patents have chronic infections. The book *Cystic Fibrosis Handbook for Patient and Family* explains:

> Once established in the lungs, [*Pseudomonas aeruginosa*] will stick to the surface of the cells lining the airways and, as a general rule, can never be wiped out. The slimy layer formed by this bacterium probably protects it from the person's normal defense mechanisms, such as white blood cells, and also likely hinders antibiotics. . . . With treatment we can control the symptoms and hope to limit tissue damage, but treatment will never completely get rid of the pseudomonas organisms in the airway.[27]

Many patients infected with pseudomonas take the antibiotic azithromycin each day because it helps improve lung function and diminishes the need for other antibiotics and hospitalizations, even though it does not cure the infection. But a study in laboratory animals reported in September 2011 suggested that using azithromycin for a long time may increase the risk of getting nontuberculous mycobacterium lung infections, so the use of this drug has become controversial. Scientists are evaluating whether this risk applies to humans, and until further research

CF patients are highly subject to lung infections. The *Pseudomonas aeruginosa* bacteria shown here are almost impossible to eradicate once established in the lungs.

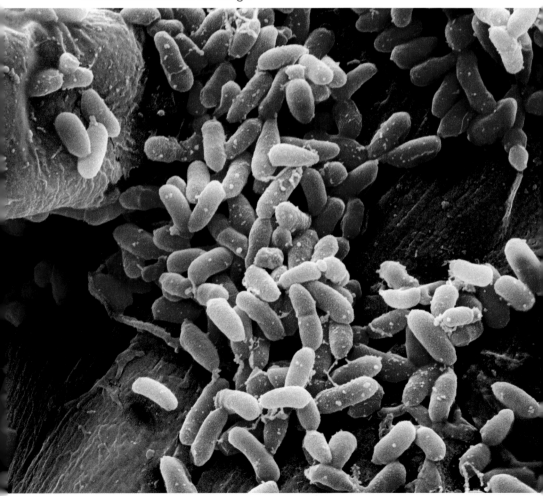

is completed, the CFF is advising patients to ask a physician whether using azithromycin is best in individual cases. A newer antibiotic, inhalable aztreonam, was approved by the U.S. Food and Drug Administration (FDA) in 2010 for use against pseudomonas, and once it becomes widely available, doctors plan to assess whether it leads to long-term improvements and can replace the use of azithromycin.

Another bacterium, *Burkholderia cepacia*, is also difficult to eradicate. Although it affects fewer patients than pseudomonas does, it can lead to a rapid deterioration of lung function. Burkholderia also spreads very easily from one person to another, so CF clinics isolate patients infected with either *Burkholderia* or *Pseudomonas* from other patients.

Other common lung infections seen in people with CF result from an allergy to the fungus *Aspergillus*. Treatment for this consists of antifungal drugs such as itraconazole and corticosteroids such as prednisone to reduce allergic inflammation. Antifungal drugs can cause liver damage and other side effects, and corticosteroids increase the risk of infections, cancer, and diabetes, so doctors try to minimize dosages and give these medications for only short periods of time.

Failing Lungs

When lung infections and lung function worsen despite treatment, patients may require continuous oxygen infusions in a hospital. If this is not helpful, the person may need a ventilator to breathe. These steps usually occur close to the end of life, and few patients survive long after this unless they receive a lung transplant. The author of *Cystic Fibrosis Handbook for Patient and Family* writes:

> As this point approaches, it's inevitable that the person and his family will consider prolonging life for days or perhaps weeks through intubation (inserting a tube into the windpipe) and using a ventilator to take over total breathing for the person. This can only be carried out in an intensive care unit, and most centers discourage this form of treatment. While intubation and artificial ventilation

may extend life for a short time, this almost never provides either physical or mental comfort for the person being treated.[28]

Some families, however, insist on supported breathing until the very end in hopes of a miracle occurring or of a donor lung becoming available if the patient is on a transplant waiting list. If a compatible donor is found, this can give a patient a second chance at life.

Doctors often place patients whom they believe are strong enough to survive a grueling lung transplant operation on a waiting list when it becomes obvious that the lungs are failing. A dire shortage of transplantable organs has led to the creation of such lists, and priority is given to desperately ill patients and to children. Despite the priority system, about one in three patients on waiting lists die before a set of donor lungs can be found.

Once a donor whose blood and tissue types closely match the CF patient is found, a transplant may proceed. Over sixteen hundred people with CF have received lung transplants since 1991. Surgeons usually transplant both lungs from a deceased donor. In rare cases lung pieces from two live donors may be used, and these pieces will regenerate into entire lungs to fill the chest cavity. But doctors rarely perform this type of procedure because it involves major surgery for three people.

About 90 percent of patients who receive a lung transplant are alive one year later, and about 50 percent are alive five years later. The operation is still very risky, and follow-up care requires patients to take immunosuppressive drugs for the rest of their lives to prevent the immune system from attacking and rejecting the new lungs, since even compatible matches are not totally accepted by the recipient's body. Even with these drugs, rejection can occur, and the drugs can have serious side effects such as an inability to fight infections and cancers. For some people, dealing with these side effects is as bad as their original condition.

Many transplant recipients, however, do well with small doses of immunosuppressives and consider any side effects to

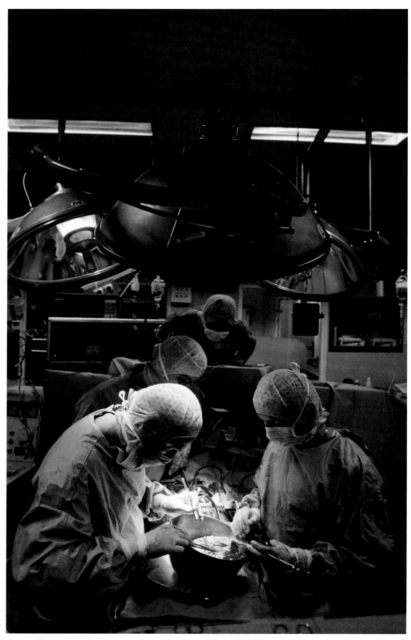

Surgeons perform a lung transplant. CF patients often seek such transplants to replace their failing lungs, but the wait for suitable donors is long and the surgical risk great.

be well worth being given a second chance to live. Although the transplant does not cure CF, a new set of lungs can allow the individual to do things he or she was previously unable to do. Isa Byrnes, who received a lung transplant at age thirty-two after being close to death, writes in the book *With Every Breath*:

> Five months after my transplant, [husband] Andrew and I hiked in the Black Hills of South Dakota at 6000 feet elevation and I participated in the 2004 US Transplant Games in Minnesota. Although I came in next to last for the 1500 meter racewalk, I ran/walked the 5K and won a gold medal for playing two matches of volleyball. . . . Though I am always wary of medication side effects and complications, I never knew I could feel so 'normal,' breathe so freely, and feel so fully alive.[29]

Other CF Treatments

Along with these ongoing and complication-ridden treatments, CF patients with other complications may require additional therapies. Those with CFRD often need insulin injections several times a day to manage their blood sugar levels. They must also do finger sticks to test blood sugar using a glucose meter several times a day, and they must be careful to keep their food intake, exercise regimen, and insulin dosages in perfect balance to avoid dangerously high or low blood sugar levels. For many people with CF, adding the need for diabetes treatment into an already intense daily treatment schedule is extremely challenging. A teen named James, for example, states, "CF has always been a part of my life so I didn't mind too much about the treatment but I hate having diabetes. The injections and blood tests are a pain. I know if I miss them I'll feel rotten, but it's hard to do every day without a break."[30]

Another common complication, nasal polyps, can make breathing difficult, so many patients use steroid nasal sprays to shrink these growths. If this does not work, doctors can remove the polyps surgically. Other respiratory complications, such as sinus infections and lung bleeds, may require surgery to clear blocked sinuses or to repair torn blood vessels in the lungs. These complications, and the need for hospitalizations, can make living with CF difficult and frustrating for patients and families, especially when coupled with time-consuming daily therapies. Most, however, are grateful that such treatments are available today, since they have been responsible for allowing patients to live into adulthood in recent years.

CHAPTER FOUR

Living with Cystic Fibrosis

Medical experts and affected families agree that living with CF is challenging and often heartbreaking. Mary Kontos, a nurse who works with CF patients, writes, "Parents would not choose this life for themselves or their child, yet must rise to the challenge of physical, emotional, and financial demands. . . . Living with CF is about faith, hope, and courage. You have to have faith that you are getting the right advice, hope that it will make a difference, and the courage to meet the challenges every day brings."[31]

Mental Stresses

Patients and parents of children with any illness face challenges, but those with a chronic, incurable disease face unique stresses and obstacles. Parents grieve from the knowledge that a child with CF will not be the carefree, healthy child they envisioned. Many also feel guilty that their genes caused the disease, even though this situation was beyond their control.

When confronted with a diagnosis of CF, many parents and patients progress through the classic stages of grief described by psychologists: shock, denial, anger, guilt, depression, and acceptance. Some, however, become stuck in one phase or another. Doctors say this is not healthy, because patients and

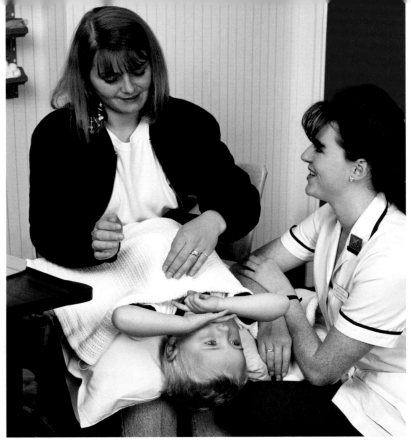

A physiologist teaches a mother exercises to help alleviate her son's CF symptoms. The treatment needs of CF patients can be stressful for both patients and caregivers.

their families must accept the reality of the disease in order to cope effectively.

People with chronic diseases typically experience higher-than-normal rates of ongoing depression and anxiety, in large part because of the stress of dealing with an illness that can have fatal complications at any time. A 2010 study at the University of Miami found that one in three CF patients aged twelve and under have high levels of anxiety, and about 11 percent are clinically depressed. Similar percentages of adult patients suffer from these conditions. In addition, about 24 percent of mothers of children with CF experience depression, and more than 50 percent report ongoing anxiety.

Researcher Alexandra Quittner states in a CFF publication that anxiety and depression are "a normal response to a very difficult situation,"[32] but that these emotional states can interfere with performing necessary treatments, since depressed or anxious people often feel hopeless and neglect themselves. Quittner recommends that CF doctors look for signs of anxiety and depression in patients and parents so psychotherapists can intervene to assist with coping, not only to improve the quality of life, but coincidentally to improve treatment compliance.

Siblings of children with CF, as well as patients and parents, may need coping assistance and reassurance. One sibling of a child with CF writes, "I, as the well sibling, through no fault of

A young woman meets with her counselor. People with CF and other chronic diseases are more susceptible to depression and anxiety because of the difficulty of dealing with an illness that could take their life at any time.

65 Roses

The name cystic fibrosis *can be difficult to pronounce, especially for children. Because the name of the disease sounds like "sixty-five roses" when spoken out loud, this has become a well-known nickname for CF. The Cystic Fibrosis Foundation explains how this came about:*

Mary G. Weiss became a volunteer for the Cystic Fibrosis Foundation in 1965 after learning that her three little boys had CF. Her duty was to call every civic club, social and service organization seeking financial support for CF research. Mary's 4-year-old son, Richard, listened closely to his mother as she made each call.

After several calls, Richard came into the room and told his Mom, "I know what you are working for." Mary was dumbstruck because Richard did not know what she was doing, nor did he know that he had cystic fibrosis. With some trepidation, Mary asked, "What am I working for, Richard?" He answered, "You are working for 65 Roses." . . .

Since 1965, the term "65 Roses" has been used by children of all ages to describe their disease.

Cystic Fibrosis Foundation. "About 65 Roses," September 19, 2006. www.cff.org/aboutCF Foundation/About65 Roses.

The Cystic Fibrosis Foundation coined the nickname Sixty-Five Roses for CF because it is easier for children to say and remember than cystic fibrosis.

anyone, often took a backseat to those who needed my parents' attention much more than I did. . . . As a child I felt left out."[33] Therefore, psychotherapists emphasize that parents should be mindful and supportive of healthy siblings as well as of the child with CF.

Factors That Contribute to Feelings of Isolation in Patients

Feeling left out is also an issue that affects CF patients, and the person's need for daily therapies or hospitalizations, which makes him or her "different" from others, often contributes to this feeling. As CF patient Lauren Bombardier writes, "I was in the hospital for my first day of first grade. . . . I spent my days in an unfamiliar room being poked and prodded by doctors while my peers learned to read and write."[34]

The unpredictable nature of CF can also cause feelings of frustration and isolation. A sudden lung infection and hospitalization can mean that normal activities are put on hold, and many times plans are broken and goals become temporarily unattainable. CF patient Bridget K. writes about how unforeseen circumstances related to her disease have forced her to develop alternative strategies for her plans: "Some days are easier than others. . . . When I can't meet all the goals I set for myself in exactly the way I'd like to, that's where the Plan B, C, D, etc. come into play. I call myself the 'Queen of Plan B' because I always have a backup plan for when life throws an obstacle in my way."[35]

For students with CF, schoolwork can suffer from these emergencies, and this is difficult for children and adolescents who want to do their best. College student Katy Seymour says in a CFF article:

> The most challenging part is being sick and missing classes. I come in contact with so many people that it's easy for me to get sick. One bad bug can land me in the hospital for several days—I have to be careful and conscious about that. The amount of work it takes to make friends and get involved on campus, coupled with everything I have

to think about with CF, makes going to college more challenging.[36]

Another school-related challenge revolves around needing to take medications and doing other "different" things that tag a person as "ill." This entails getting permission to take medication and perhaps to leave class, as well as dealing with other kids' reactions to someone who is different. A young child's parents are responsible for informing teachers and school administrators about a child's needs, and many parents are quick to intervene if these needs are not met. These younger children, however, still face being teased about being sick or scrawny. Adolescents who prefer to take on these responsibilities and surmount any hurdles themselves are faced not only with feeling different from peers, but also with battling administrators to have their needs met. A teen named Jamie explains: "The transition from middle school to high school was a big trek for me, particularly with CF to carry. I had a handful of new teachers to explain my disease to, and I also had to face different rules enforced by this new school that sometimes conflicted with my

A CF patient uses a nebulizer to help her breathe. Having CF means having a lifestyle centered around a chronic disease, which can make patients feel isolated and different.

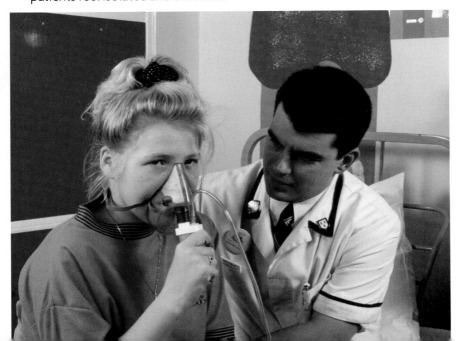

needs. As important as it was to make the school's faculty under-stand my situation, it wasn't always easy."[37]

Jamie needed doctors' notes to allow him to leave class when he had to cough, get a drink, or rest in the nurse's office. Although the school had a no-water-bottle policy, Jamie got permission to carry a water bottle so he could stay hydrated, especially in hot weather or when he was taking intravenous antibiotics. These exceptions led to teasing and bullying from other kids and resistance from teachers who believed he was taking advantage of his permission to leave class.

Challenges for Adults

Since more and more CF patients are living into adulthood, the challenges of living with the disease now follow people into the workplace as well as to school. According to a CFF publication, "Career choices should be based primarily on each individual's intellect, ability, interests and life goals. People with CF are not limited in choice of employment and enjoy success in a wide variety of professional, technical, clerical and blue collar jobs."[38] Despite these assertions, CF does limit some career options and can affect an individual's ability to reliably show up for work when emergencies arise. Doctors say it is best for patients to do work that offers flexible hours so they can take time off for treatments or hospitalizations. Most people with CF tire easily, which limits their ability to engage in strenuous occupations that require physical labor. Doctors recommend that people with CF also avoid working in environments with smoke, dust, paints, or chemicals that can irritate the lungs. They also should not work with babies or children, since young ones frequently get and pass around colds. Careers that expose people to high altitudes (such as airline pilot or park ranger) are also not recommended because low oxygen levels in these conditions can cause blood oxygen levels to drop.

Legally, people do not have to share information about an illness with an employer unless the condition requires special accommodations. Most CF patients do not disclose their illness during a job interview, but many do tell the employer about it once they have been hired. Experts say this is a personal decision. Although the Americans with Disabilities Act prohibits discrimination based on medical status, bias still exists and can result in being fired from a job. Thus, many people are wary of mentioning their illness.

Another issue that commonly affects adults with CF is whether or not to reproduce or adopt children. Most individuals with CF are infertile, but techniques such as sperm retrieval for men or fertility treatments for women can make it possible to conceive a baby. Pregnancy, however, tends to worsen CF and increases the chances of a woman developing CFRD or lung infections, so most doctors advise against it. Some parents who have CF choose to adopt children, but many do not because the disease shortens and disrupts their lives so much that others would likely have to step in and care for the children.

Most CF carriers also elect not to have biological children because of the risks that any offspring would either be a carrier or have CF, but many choose to adopt children without the disease. Some carriers who wish to have a biological child undergo genetic testing on an embryo or fetus after becoming pregnant, and some then choose to terminate the pregnancy if the baby will be born with CF. Others carry the baby to term and deal with the illness.

Overcoming Challenges

Despite the challenges for people of all ages, many do not allow CF to keep them from living active, productive, fulfilling lives. Factors that strongly influence the ability to live well with CF are accepting the disease, having a positive attitude, and learning to control those things in life that can be controlled. Teenager Katherine Russell explains, "I was born with a disease. I couldn't prevent that. I can, however, prevent getting discouraged or torn apart because of the little bad things CF brings. In other words, something that will indubitably alter the effect our disease has on us is our attitude, which is why we should always try our hardest to stay positive. Keep smiling, laughing, and hoping." Russell states that sometimes it is difficult not to become discouraged and feel overwhelmed

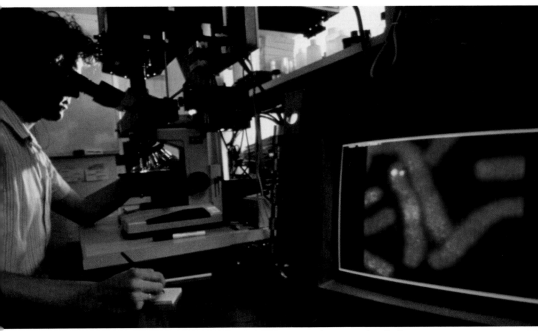

A researcher maps the genome of an embryo to look for genetic defects. Because dealing with CF is such a challenge, some parents-to-be may end a pregnancy if their fetus's genome shows a probability of CF.

when her condition worsens or when others say mean things to her, but she strives to overcome these setbacks: "People can be cold and say hurtful things, but I myself have had to learn to rise above these remarks, keep my confidence, and move on."[39]

A positive attitude and willingness to accept the need for daily treatments has also helped Aaron Stocks, who writes:

I find that managing my perspective on the disease helps me feel my best. I met an adult with CF when I was young and he gave me the best tip: "Consider yourself lucky to have CF, because you will learn to cherish life much earlier than most others come to this realization." . . . Those four hours that I take to manage my CF care are critical for me to stay healthy. When I'm not working, I try to combine activities. I'm a big fan of the Madden football video game, and I have timed it out so that I can finish a game by the time I have completed all of my nebulizers. This way, I actually look forward to doing my treatments.[40]

For children with CF, attitude is also important, and doctors say that the parents' attitude strongly influences the child's acceptance of the disease and willingness to stick with treatments. Some children manipulate their parents into feeling sorry for them and into not insisting that they take the necessary daily therapies, but doctors believe this is a mistake on the

Losing a Child to CF

Families affected by CF live with the threat of death constantly hanging over them. When a patient, particularly a child, dies from the disease, coping with the resulting grief can be overwhelming for all. One couple, Marc and Margarete Cassalina, lost their thirteen-year-old daughter, Jena, to CF in 2007. In a CFF article, they shared the story of how remembering Jena's positive attitude and being CF advocates helps them cope. The Cassalinas are CFF volunteers and have spoken to the U.S. Congress about the importance of providing funding for CF research and patient care. They are hoping that their efforts will help their son, Eric, who also has CF, and others with the disease live longer and better lives. As Margarete states:

The determination and spirit Jena had are always with me now. . . . We repeat to ourselves a quote Jena had written down for herself, "Pain is not a valid reason for stopping." No matter how much emotional pain we're going through, it's just not a valid reason for stopping our mission to help others and find a cure for CF. We also have Eric, which makes the fight that much more vital to continue.

Quoted in Cystic Fibrosis Foundation. "One on One: Marc and Margarete Cassalina." www.cff.org/ECommitment/2007_fall/people/one_on_one-Marc_and_margarete _cassalina.html.

parents' part. Instead, they advise parents to convey the attitude that daily treatments are absolutely necessary so the child can live the best possible life. Making physiotherapy fun can often help with this process. The authors of *The Facts: Cystic Fibrosis* write:

> It is useful to try to make physiotherapy time a special individual time for parent and child together rather than a daily chore. Using blowing games, for example bubbles, noisy blowing toys, incorporating play—the child as a wheelbarrow for chest drainage—tickling and laughing to encourage deep breaths and coughs, and using favourite videos or storytelling can make physio time special.[41]

Careful but Not Overprotective

While experts advise parents to be strict about incorporating treatments into the daily schedule, they also caution that it is important to allow kids to be kids at other times to prevent them from becoming fearful and resentful. Balancing the need to protect a child with CF from getting viruses or becoming overtired with allowing him to live fully can be difficult. The same need for balance applies to adults with the disease as well. Doctors suggest that becoming educated about all aspects of CF is critical in teaching parents and patients of all ages to recognize early symptoms that indicate worsening lung function or other complications. When symptoms are recognized, action can be taken to address the problem before it becomes serious. Communicating often and openly with the patient's professional care team is an important part of this monitoring process, and these measures can help with balancing the need to be cautious with the need to be active and engaged in life.

Bob Esparza, father of a son with CF, writes that it took a while for him and his wife to strike a healthy balance between being overprotective and allowing their son to thrive:

> For the first six months after the diagnosis, we were very protective of Tyler; it was like he was in a bubble. We told

the staff at school, and we brought in pamphlets about CF. We bought umpteen bottles of hand sanitizer, and we asked his teacher to keep away any kid who had a cold. We tried everything to keep him protected. But we realized we were scaring him . . . so we started to ease off. We realized there's a difference between living with the disease and living your life.[42]

Many parents of children with CF also balance caution and overprotection by encouraging participation in sports and other exercise, while monitoring their child for exhaustion. While regular exercise is important in helping people with CF live a full life, strenuous exercise can be dangerous if they push too hard and have trouble breathing.

Support Groups and Advocacy

One valuable method of learning about imposing limits and balance and finding out what works for most patients is participating in support groups with other people dealing with the disease. People in support groups share advice, experiences, and compassion that those who do not live with CF generally cannot offer. Many participants find that they gain confidence and strength from the support of others, plus they feel good about being able to extend a helping hand to group members who are experiencing familiar problems.

Support groups can meet in person or online. Some are sponsored by foundations like the CFF or by hospitals, while others are independent local groups. Facilitators lead some groups, and patients or families lead others.

Sometimes doctors advise patients not to participate in support groups because of the danger of catching lung infections from other people with CF. But most groups have strict rules about not allowing people with active infections to attend meetings, and this limits exposure to dangerous germs.

Many of those who suffer from CF find that participating in advocacy groups can also enrich their lives. Sometimes support groups participate in CF advocacy to increase public awareness, raise research funds, and lobby lawmakers for government

Claire Wineland's Foundation

In 2010 thirteen-year-old Claire Wineland nearly died from a severe lung infection and lung failure following a simple surgery. After miraculously emerging from a sixteen-day coma, Claire launched the nonprofit Claire's Place Foundation to help and inspire others affected by CF. Part of her inspiration for starting the foundation came from the thousands of people who prayed for her and helped her family during the ordeal.

Claire writes a blog, creates videos, and puts together events such as flash mobs where people dance to raise funds for CF care and research. She has gotten celebrities such as Michael J. Fox, Tracy Pollan, and Counting Crows lead singer Adam Duritz involved, and one of her flash mobs in Los Angeles raised twenty-four thousand dollars in May 2011 to help families cover the costs of caring for children with CF. Her future plans include publishing a book of essays to show CF patients that all is not hopeless. The Claire's Place Foundation website states, "Claire's Place Foundation is a way for Claire to give back and make meaning of what she has had to go through; the foundation is her way to enrich the human experience with hope, strength, and joy."

Claire's Place Foundation. "About Claire." http://clairesplacefoundation.org/about-claire.

funding and support of programs that benefit people with the disease. Other times, patients and families volunteer in advocacy organizations on their own. Lovisa McCallum, mother of a son who has CF, is one volunteer and advocate who derives great satisfaction from her efforts. She states in a Cystic Fibrosis Canada article, "Volunteering gives me a sense of empowerment. My son has a genetic illness that I couldn't have prevented and that I am not medically capable of fixing. But, I can put my actions where my dreams are and volunteer. I do everything I can to help us get closer to a cure."[43]

Many advocates are everyday people helping to make a difference, and some are celebrities who use their fame to help raise

Many celebrities use their fame to help raise funds for and awareness about CF. Canadian singer Celine Dion, who lost her niece to CF, has raised funds for the Canadian Cystic Fibrosis Foundation.

funds and awareness. Singer Celine Dion, whose niece Karine died of CF at age sixteen, has helped the Canadian Cystic Fibrosis Foundation and has performed in numerous benefit concerts to support CF research. Former National Football League quarterback Boomer Esiason started the Boomer Esiason Foundation after his son, Gunnar, was diagnosed with CF in 1993. The foundation raises research funds and provides support, scholarships, and financial assistance to families affected by CF. Its Team Boomer program encourages people with CF to exercise and calls on athletes in all sports to participate in fund-raising races. In explaining why he started the foundation, Esiason writes, "One of the first lessons I learned in youth football was that winning requires all of the individual athletes on a team to come together, to cooperate and to support each other. It's a lesson I think also applies to cystic fibrosis."[44]

One important result of support and advocacy efforts is that they help people affected by CF keep up their hopes for the future to bring improvements in life span, quality of life, and eventually a cure. As Donna O'Neill, the parent of a child with CF and an avid fund-raiser for CF research and advocacy programs, states in a newspaper article, "Every day we fight for our children's health and we dream of a day where 'CF' stands for 'Cure Found.'"[45]

CHAPTER FIVE

The Future

Since cystic fibrosis continues to impose great hardships for patients and families and still results in premature death, advocates and researchers are engaged in efforts to improve awareness and treatment and eventually find a cure. Since CF does not affect as many people as many other severe diseases do, most private drug and research companies, as well as the U.S. government's National Institutes of Health (NIH), which funds most medical research in this country, have been reluctant to devote large sums of money to CF research and patient benefits. However, CF advocates and organizations like the CFF have been successful in raising money for these purposes and are constantly striving to convince lawmakers to increase funding. Much research that focuses on developing new and better treatments, on finding a cure, and on improving diagnosis and treatment compliance is currently under way.

Research on Improving Treatment Compliance

Many CF patients do not stick to a treatment plan, so several studies are exploring methods of improving treatment compliance. Adolescents are especially likely to skip their therapies, so a company called Dawkins Productions is collaborating with researchers at several hospitals to encourage teens to take better

Many programs have been developed to help CF patients, especially adolescents, to maintain their lifelong treatment protocols.

care of themselves. They have developed a cell phone application called CFFONE: A Cell Phone Support Program for Adolescents with Cystic Fibrosis and are using social networking to help with disease management. According to the investigators, CFFONE

> will make use of cutting-edge technology—a broadband capable, cellular telephone keyed into a highly-interactive informational web site. This web site will provide engaging

online learning activities and resources specific to adolescents with cystic fibrosis. We believe the information and activities contained in CFFONE will improve adolescents' knowledge, attitudes, and practices around cystic fibrosis and that adolescents exposed to the CFFONE program will demonstrate an increase in adherence to their treatment regimens and related improvements in their health status and quality of life.[46]

Another experimental program, the I Change Adherence and Raise Expectations (iCARE) study being conducted by Novartis Pharmaceuticals, is addressing treatment compliance in adults and adolescents. Half the research centers involved in the study will use the Comprehensive Adherence Program (CAP) for two years. CAP uses a web-based program called the Adherence Dashboard that gives patients regular automated updates on whether or not they are refilling their medications on schedule, plus incorporates a training program known as CF My Way. This program teaches problem-solving skills to help patients stick to treatment. The other half of the research centers in the iCARE study will use only the Adherence Dashboard in the first year and CAP in the second year. The researchers will then compare medication refill compliance, lung function, and overall quality of life in patients in both groups.

Improved Monitoring

Other research on improving patient care centers on teaching patients to do daily home monitoring of their condition. Doctors at Johns Hopkins University are testing a program in which one group of patients performs daily lung function tests with a spirometer and transmits the results to doctors on a weekly basis. A second group does not monitor lung function at home, but receives CF education and is taught to recognize early warning signs of worsening lung disease. This group is encouraged to call a study nurse immediately if they experience such symptoms.

The objective in both groups is to catch worsening lung disease early on so aggressive treatment can be started. The researchers will compare health and quality of life improvements in both groups to see which monitoring program is most effective.

Other studies on improving CF monitoring are looking for better laboratory methods of detecting worsening lung function. Several research teams are searching for biomarkers (chemicals in the blood that can be used to assess the presence or worsening of a disease) that reliably predict worsening lung function before symptoms appear. Scientists at Oregon Health

A CF patient monitors and treats her condition at home. Improved monitoring programs are allowing CF patients to live longer.

and Science University, for example, are investigating whether
levels of co-stimulatory molecules can serve as biomarkers.
Co-stimulatory molecules play a role in stimulating and activating immune cells. Thus, their presence may indicate worsening
lung inflammation.

Other body chemicals that may play a role in lung inflammation are sex hormones, which become active during adolescence. Some doctors believe that monitoring sex hormone
levels and finding out how they affect inflammation may offer
yet another method of helping physicians prevent and treat
worsening lung function. Researchers led by Neil Sweezey at
the Hospital for Sick Children in Toronto, Canada, have found
that the female hormone estrogen affects several chemicals in
the airways of CF patients, and they are attempting to determine how this impacts airway inflammation. Several other studies have determined that in general, females with CF are more
susceptible to serious lung infections than males are, and the
Canadian researchers are trying to find out the reasons for this
as well. According to the Canadian Cystic Fibrosis Foundation:

> Dr. Sweezey has found that high levels of the female sex hor-
> mone, estrogen, reduce the immune system's ability to fight
> infection by the bacterium P. aeruginosa, and increase harm-
> ful lung inflammation. Dr. Sweezey will examine whether
> the other female sex hormone, progesterone, is also in-
> volved in increased infection and inflammation and whether
> inhaled hormone-blocking drugs are able to prevent the
> harmful effects caused by these hormones.[47]

Other researchers are evaluating the effects of male hormones
on CF.

Efforts to Reduce Complications

Other efforts to understand and reduce lung inflammation and
infection are focusing on studying the bacteria that plague CF
patients. Scientists at Children's Hospital Boston are studying
a newly recognized characteristic of these bacteria: bacteria com-
munities. As the researchers write:

Scientists have begun to realize that many types of bacteria often live together as a complex community, and the investigators wish to apply that idea to the bacteria in the respiratory system of people with Cystic Fibrosis (CF). It is possible that the survival of the many millions of bacteria in the CF lung depends on the production of special chemicals that might be made only by very few types of bacteria. If that is true, medicines that interfere with those chemicals could treat the lung infections that cause trouble for nearly all people with CF.[48]

A young CF patient has his lung function monitored. Scientists are studying the bacteria that cause lung infections in CF patients to see whether breathing complications can be minimized.

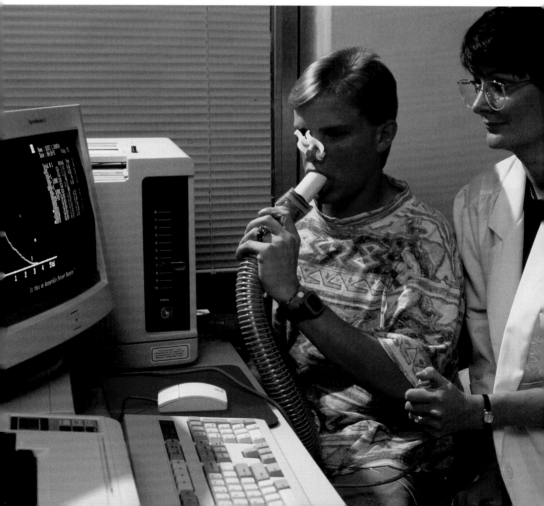

Research into Making Diagnosis Easier

Some research efforts are directed at making diagnosis easier and faster. Researchers at Polychrome Medical are testing a new product that may improve sweat tests. Currently, doctors must collect sweat in tubing or on gauze filter paper and analyze it using a chloridometer machine that measures chloride content. The new product, known as the CF Quantum Sweat Test System, uses a chloride test patch to collect and analyze sweat and does not require other laboratory equipment. It also requires far less sweat than other methods do, and doctors believe this will be especially helpful in testing infants, who often do not produce enough sweat for traditional sweat tests. Scientists are now comparing results obtained with the Quantum to those with traditional tests to assess how reliable the new test is.

Another research project is testing a new method of diagnosing CF in people with mild cases, in which it is sometimes difficult to reach a definitive diagnosis. Researchers at Children's Hospital of Philadelphia are using a technique called nasal transepithelial potential difference (NPD) to assess whether dripping solutions containing sodium and chloride into the nose and measuring how well these solutions move across nasal cell membranes can reliably diagnose CF. Scientists currently use NPD to assess how well new treatments repair the defective sodium and chloride ion movement that characterizes CF.

Additional research on complications is looking at ways of preventing some of the other common problems that affect people with CF—primarily CFRD. Two CFRD-prevention studies are based on previous research at Emory University in Atlanta, which indicated that high blood sugar levels lead to high levels of cytokines (chemicals that increase inflammation), and that these cytokines and the inflammation they cause are toxic to beta cells and may indeed be responsible for full-blown diabetes.

In one study, researchers at Hadassah Medical Organization in Israel are evaluating whether administering insulin injections to patients with worsening lung disease will protect beta cells in the pancreas and therefore prevent CFRD. CF patients are more likely to develop CFRD during serious lung infections, and the scientists believe that injecting insulin may offset this process by preventing beta cells from being exposed to high blood sugar levels, which can destroy these cells.

In a related study, researchers at the University of British Columbia are trying to prevent CFRD with the oral drug sitagliptin. This medication increases the level of chemicals in the body that lower blood sugar. It is often used to treat people whose bodies produce insulin but who are insulin resistant. The investigators are hoping that lowering blood sugar levels in this way will protect beta cells so that patients will not go on to develop CFRD and require ongoing insulin injections.

Research on Drug Treatments

In addition to investigating methods of preventing certain complications, many researchers are testing new and better treatments for CF itself. Scientists develop new drugs in a laboratory and initially test them for safety and effectiveness on laboratory animals. If a drug passes these tests, a drug company may apply to the FDA for permission to test it on human volunteers in clinical trials. These trials begin with preliminary phases that test the drug on a small number of patients to establish safe, effective doses. In later phases the drug is given to large numbers of people, and results are compared with results obtained with a placebo (a fake that looks like the real thing). Researchers use placebos so that any positive effects can be attributed to the drug itself rather than to the expectation of success.

One challenge that scientists face when testing new drugs is finding enough people to participate in clinical trials. This is especially true in diseases that affect children, since parents are often reluctant to expose their child to the risk of taking an

unproven medication. However, doctors point out that the up-
side of participation is that patients will have early access to a
promising treatment, and they can potentially help many other
patients if the drug is approved. Advocacy organizations encourage parents and patients to weigh carefully the possible
risks and benefits of participating in a drug study. As the CFF
points out, "Without patient volunteers, research and progress
are not possible."[49]

Drugs Being Tested

There are many new CF drugs currently being tested. Since
pseudomonas infections are particularly difficult to defeat for
those with CF, many scientists are evaluating medications to
control this bacterium. Researchers funded by the CFF are
testing an intravenous drug called gallium nitrate (brand name
Ganite), which reduces the amount of calcium in the body. It is
currently used to treat high levels of calcium that result from
some forms of cancer. Gallium has also been found to kill certain bacteria, and the researchers hope it will be effective
against pseudomonas. However, this drug has serious side effects such as kidney and heart damage, so if it proves to be effective, it would only be used in CF patients for whom less
toxic drugs do not work.

Another anti-pseudomonas drug being tested is an antibody
(an immune chemical that attacks a particular organism)
called anti-pseudomonas IgY. IgY is administered by gargling
liquid containing the antibody in the throat and spitting out the
solution, much like people gargle mouthwash. Scientists make
anti-pseudomonas IgY by vaccinating hens with pseudomonas
and extracting the antibody the hens' bodies produce. Preliminary results indicate that patients who gargle with IgY daily do
not get as many pseudomonas infections as do those who only
receive antibiotics.

New forms of antibiotics, such as inhaled MP-376, or Aero-
quin, are also being tested against pseudomonas. MP-376 is a
new inhalable form of the oral antibiotic levofloxacin. Doctors
believe the inhaled form of the antibiotic will be more aggressive than the oral form.

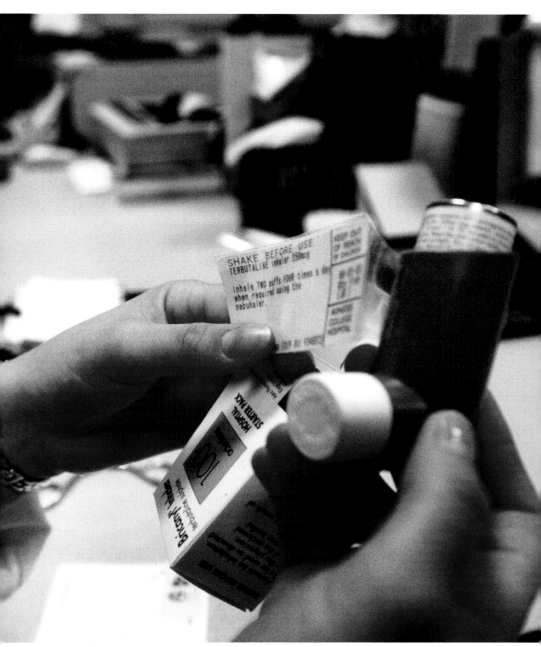

A pharmacist holds one of several new handheld antibiotic inhalers. New handheld inhalers could revolutionize the way CF patients are able to take their medicine, making it more convenient.

Gene Modifiers

Other drugs being tested seek to reverse the effects of the gene mutations that cause CF. The FDA approved Vertex Pharmaceuticals' new drug Kalydeco, which is the first medication to address the root causes of CF, in early 2012. This drug targets only one of the many *CFTR* mutations—the G551D mutation, which affects about 4 percent of CF patients, so similar drugs are being tested as well. The G551D mutation allows a defective CFTR protein to form, but the protein blocks chloride ion channels on cell membranes. Kalydeco fixes the defective protein and unblocks these channels.

Clinical trial data showed that Kalydeco leads to more than a 10 percent improvement in lung function in many patients, which scientist Bonnie Ramsey told the *New York Times* "are amazing results."[50] Patients in the trials also gained weight, and sweat tests revealed that their sweat became less salty. There were some side effects, such as headache, rashes, dizziness, and nasal congestion, but doctors do not consider these effects to be serious. CF advocates thus far see the main drawback of Kalydeco as its cost of almost three hundred thousand dollars per patient per year. Pharmaceutical companies claim they must charge large amounts for these types of drugs because of the immense costs of developing the medications.

Vertex is also testing two other new drugs, VX-809 and VX-661, which target the most common *CFTR* mutation, deltaF508. Both VX-809 and VX-661 seem to work best when given in combination with Kalydeco. Studies are now evaluating the safety and effectiveness of various doses of both drugs when given alone and in combination with Kalydeco. VX-809 and VX-661 correct the deltaF508 mutation by allowing the defective CFTR protein to move to its proper place on cell membranes so chloride ion channels can open.

Researchers at Hadassah Medical Organization are testing several other new gene modifiers. Preliminary results show that one drug, ataluren, lets the CFTR protein function more normally and improves lung function in patients who have a nonsense *CFTR* mutation. Nonsense mutations interrupt the

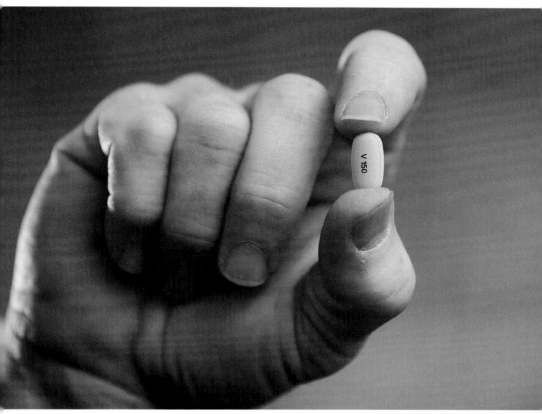

Vertex Pharmaceuticals's newly approved drug Kalydeco (shown) is the first medication to address the root cause of CF by targeting a specific gene mutation.

production of the CFTR protein so it ends up being too short to work properly. About 10 percent of CF patients have nonsense mutations. Ataluren allows a complete protein to be manufactured.

Other new drugs, epigallocatechin gallate (EGCG) and tocotrienol, correct *CFTR* splicing mutations. Splicing mutations result from DNA sequences failing to be hooked together in the correct order. This leads to the production of incomplete CFTR proteins. Given separately or together, EGCG and tocotrienol appear to allow complete proteins to be manufactured, and the Israeli researchers are now testing the safety of these treatments.

Existing Drugs Being Tested

In addition to experimenting with new drugs, many researchers are testing medications already approved for other purposes. The antibiotic doxycycline, for example, is used to treat infections other than lung infections, but evidence that it decreases inflammation has led scientists to begin evaluating whether it reduces lung inflammation in CF patients. The cholesterol-lowering drug simvastatin also seems to decrease inflammation, and researchers are assessing whether it is helpful in reducing lung inflammation as well.

Several safe, natural substances are also being evaluated for use in treating CF. A sweetener called xylitol, commonly used in sugarless gum, seems to prevent bacterial growth and lower the salt content in the airways of people with CF. Researchers at the

Scientists at Emory University are studying whether vitamin D supplements enhance the immune system's ability to fight lung infections.

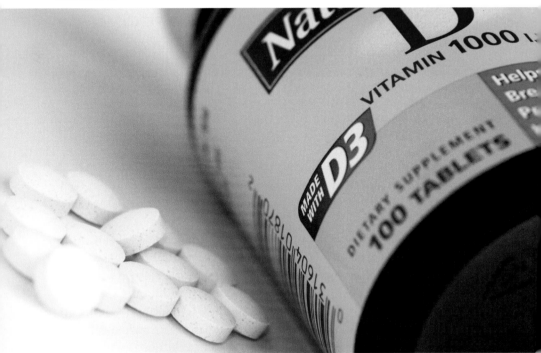

University of Iowa are testing whether inhaled xylitol is effective for this purpose.

Another natural substance, ghrelin, stimulates appetite and may possibly decrease inflammation. According to researchers at Papworth Hospital in England, "Reduced body weight is associated with increased inflammatory lung damage and is a major predictor of mortality [death] in CF patients. . . . A therapy which improves nutrition may therefore have a significant effect on the prognosis of this disease."[51] The researchers are injecting test patients with ghrelin and assessing improvements in eating and weight gain and reductions in immune cell inflammation.

Although some people with CF already take vitamin D supplements, many do not, and doctors believe a lack of this vitamin may lead to worsening lung infections. Thus, scientists at Emory University in Atlanta are studying whether vitamin D supplements enhance the immune system's ability to fight lung infections. The researchers write, "New research has suggested that high levels of vitamin D may be protective against lung infections and may promote the actions of anti-bacterial proteins needed to ward off infections. Research has also suggested that high vitamin D levels are linked to lower mortality rates; however these hypotheses have not been adequately studied in patients with CF."[52]

Toward a Cure

While efforts to improve treatment with medications continue, the ultimate research goal—a cure—is also being explored. Experts agree that the most likely cure will involve using gene therapy to permanently replace or repair the faulty genes that cause CF. Thus far, however, no one has perfected methods of achieving this goal. Scientists have been experimenting with gene therapy for many genetic diseases since the 1980s, but several tragic events slowed research progress immensely. In 1999 a young man named Jesse Gelsinger died after receiving gene therapy for a rare liver disease, and in 2003 several children with an immune disease developed leukemia after genes inserted to replace faulty genes activated cancer genes in their cells. After these events, new regulations forced gene therapy studies to proceed slowly and more cautiously.

Replacing mutated genes can be accomplished using several methods. The most common uses a vector, or carrier, to carry normal genes into cells. Modified viruses that have been rendered incapable of causing infections are usually used as vectors since viruses by nature have the ability to enter and infect cells. Adenoviruses, adeno-associated viruses, and retroviruses have all been used as vectors. Different types of viruses are better equipped to enter different types of cells.

The normal genes and vectors are introduced into a patient by injection or by the person inhaling them. But often the vector is inefficient at getting the genes into cells, the person's immune system attacks the vector, or even though the viral vector is modified so as not to cause disease, it sometimes alters the cell's DNA and causes cancer.

In 1990 scientists succeeded in adding normal copies of the *CFTR* gene to lung cells grown in a laboratory. Then in 1993 researchers modified a common adenovirus that causes colds to act as a vector to deliver normal genes to the lungs of CF patients. However, the vectors failed to deliver enough working copies of the gene to correct the symptoms of CF. Doctors tried administering higher doses of the vector/gene, but the patients' immune systems attacked the combination. In 1995 scientists tried using a liposome (fat capsule) vector, but the fat capsules did not get into the cells and also caused fever and inflammation in some patients.

Rather than using adenovirus or liposome vectors, other scientists have tried using adeno-associated viruses, which do not cause diseases in humans. However, these viruses are tiny and cannot carry much DNA with them. They also do not penetrate cells easily. But since adeno-associated viruses do not seem to trigger an immune response in people, scientists are pursuing new methods of using them. In 2009 researchers at the University of California–Berkeley and the University of Iowa made progress in this method when they turned an adeno-associated virus into an infectious virus that easily penetrated lung cells in laboratory cultures. The researchers are now testing the new vector in pigs that are genetically engineered to have CF in hopes that the gene mutation can be corrected. If this proves to be safe and effective, they will proceed with human testing.

The Berkeley-Iowa team has also developed new methods for forcing viruses to evolve into forms that the human immune system will not attack. These techniques are known as "directed evolution." They may prove to be helpful in creating vectors that can remain in the human body for long periods of time without being destroyed, giving them time to correct genetic mutations. One of the Berkeley researchers, David Schaffer, states in a news article, "We devised a way to evolve viruses that are released of the natural constraints of evolution and have the freedom or ability to evolve toward properties that are more useful for medical application. In human lung tissue, it completely rescued the chloride ion transport properties of cells after delivering the correct copy of the CFTR gene to replace the mutated copy."[53] These manipulated viruses could eventually be a powerful tool in the fight against CF.

Other Gene Therapy Techniques

Because vectors have thus far not proved to be safe and effective, researchers are also exploring other methods of replacing or repairing mutated genes. Some experimenters are attempting to place an extra chromosome into target cells. The artificial chromosome would carry the desired genetic information and would probably not be attacked by the immune system. However, figuring out how to introduce such a large molecule into a cell has been challenging.

Other scientists are exploring methods of swapping a normal gene for a mutated one using homologous recombination. Here, a normal gene is inserted into a cell with a molecule that directs it to find a certain DNA sequence and take its place. This method has yet to be perfected.

Scientists are also testing techniques that work by transmitting instructions to repair defective genes. One technique, called selective reverse mutation, would insert DNA sequences into a cell that instruct a defective gene to repair itself. A related method, called spliceosome-mediated RNA trans-splicing

Teen Wins Research Award

In May 2011 sixteen-year-old Marshall Zhang of Toronto, Canada, won first place in the Sanofi-Aventis Bio Talent challenge for original research by a teenager. Zhang used the Canadian SCINET superconducting network (a computer system that simulates, or models, real-life chemical effects) to investigate how two chemical compounds act to correct defective CFTR proteins. He found that each compound acted against different parts of the protein, and later he tested living cells to see whether the computer simulation results held true. Zhang told Fox News that the two compounds "actually worked together in creating an effect that was greater than the sum of its parts." In other words, using both compounds together was much more effective than using either alone.

Zhang and the scientists who mentored him at the Hospital for Sick Children believe these findings are a major breakthrough, even though the compounds may prove to be ineffective or toxic if given to people with CF. "I have identified certain chemical structures that are key in the corrective effects of these molecules, as well as identified two molecular targets on the protein for future therapeutics," Zhang stated.

Quoted in Fox News. "Teen Discovers Promising Cystic Fibrosis Treatment," May 13, 2011. www.foxnews.com/health/2011/05/13/teen-discovers-promising-cystic-fibrosis-treatment.

(SMaRT), was pioneered by scientists at the University of Iowa in 2001. Using the SMaRT system, researchers first inserted a decoy gene sequence known as a minigene into diseased human lung cells' DNA to tell the cells to correct the faulty instructions issued by mutated *CFTR* genes. The decoy sequence actually acts on the cells' RNA, which translates the DNA code. Cells copy DNA instructions onto an RNA strand, then "read" the instructions from the RNA.

The researchers used a machine called a spliceosome to slice up the cell's RNA and paste it back together while incorporating the new minigene. They then implanted the cells into mice and found that the cells began manufacturing a normal CFTR protein for a while. However, the cells soon stopped following the minigene's instructions. Scientists are attempting to overcome this problem with further research.

Outlook for the Future

Even with research on improving treatments and curing CF under way, medical experts agree that there is still much to do before patients can look forward to a normal life and life span. Thousands of patients and families who live with CF are hoping that a cure will be found sooner rather than later. As CF advocate Margarete Cassalina, who lost her daughter, Jena, to CF and has a son with the disease, states in a CFF article, "We don't have time to lose. We needed this cure yesterday."[54]

But realistically, states CF expert Preston W. Campbell III of Johns Hopkins Hospital in a *New York Times* article, "I think it's unlikely that in the next 20 years we will have a treatment that is a one-time fix. It is going to be more like asthma, where patients must take medications for the rest of their lives but rarely die from their disease because they can control it. We hope that, in time, it will be the same story with cystic fibrosis."[55]

The primary goals for the immediate future are to further improve understanding and treatment of CF so the trend of more and more patients living into adulthood and even into old age continues to grow. The mission statement of the Cystic Fibrosis Foundation, "Adding Tomorrows Every Day,"[56] aptly expresses these goals and the hopes of affected people for a brighter future.

Notes

Introduction: Extending Life: A Success Story

1. Cystic Fibrosis Foundation. "Frequently Asked Questions." www.cff.org/AboutCF/Faqs.
2. Cystic Fibrosis Foundation. "About Cystic Fibrosis." www.cff.org/AboutCF.
3. Quoted in Katherine Russell and Margot Russell. *With Every Breath*. Kenmore, NY: Merrill, 2006, p. 30.
4. Albert Lowenfels and Nicholas J. Simmonds. "Cystic Fibrosis: No Longer a Disease of Childhood and Adolescence." Medscape, February 18, 2010. www.medscape.com/viewarticle/716815.

Chapter One: What Is Cystic Fibrosis?

5. Quoted in National Jewish Health. "Cystic Fibrosis: History." www.nationaljewish.org/healthinfo/conditions/cystic fibrosis/history.
6. Cystic Fibrosis Medicine. "The History of Cystic Fibrosis." www.cfmedicine.com/history/fifties.htm.
7. National Institutes of Health. "A Breakdown in Breathing." http://newsinhealth.nih.gov/issue/Jul2011/Feature2.
8. Cystic Fibrosis Foundation. "Staying Healthy." www.cff.org/LivingWithCF/StayingHealthy.
9. Daniel Markovich. *Cystic Fibrosis Handbook for Patient and Family*. London: Emjays Graphics, 2008, p. 87.
10. Jerry A. Nick and David M. Rodman. "Manifestations of Cystic Fibrosis Diagnosed in Adulthood." *Current Opinion in Pulmonary Medicine*, November 1, 2005, p. 513.
11. Anne H. Thomson and Ann Harris. *The Facts: Cystic Fibrosis*. New York: Oxford University Press, 2008, p. 6.

Chapter Two: What Causes Cystic Fibrosis?

12. Paul M. Quinton. "Physiological Basis of Cystic Fibrosis: A Historical Perspective." *Physiological Reviews*, January 1999, p. S12.
13. Howard Hughes Medical Institute. "Stalking a Lethal Gene: Finding the Faulty Gene's Fellow Travelers." www.hhmi.org/genetictrail/a110.html.
14. Howard Hughes Medical Institute. "Stalking a Lethal Gene: 'Jumping' Toward the Gene."
15. Howard Hughes Medical Institute. "Stalking A Lethal Gene: 'Jumping' Toward the Gene."
16. Markovich. *Cystic Fibrosis Handbook for Patient and Family*, p. 21.
17. J. de Gracia et al. "Genotype-Phenotype Correlation for Pulmonary Function in Cystic Fibrosis." *Thorax*, vol. 60, 2005, p. 562.
18. Clinical Trials.gov. "Gene Modifiers of Cystic Fibrosis Lung Disease." http://clinicaltrials.gov/ct2/show/NCT00037765?recr=Open&cond=%22Cystic+Fibrosis%22&rank=79.

Chapter Three: Cystic Fibrosis Treatment

19. Quoted in Cystic Fibrosis Medicine. "The History of Cystic Fibrosis."
20. Quoted in Cystic Fibrosis Foundation. "Be a Care Team Player!" www.cff.org/aboutCFFoundation/Publications/connections/archive/July2010/Be-A-Care-Team-Player.cfm.
21. Thomson and Harris. *The Facts*, pp. 37–38.
22. Quoted in Cystic Fibrosis Foundation. "Supporting Nutrition: Understanding Tube Feeding." www.cff.org/UploadedFiles/treatments/Therapies/Nutrition/TubeFeeding/Supporting%20Nutrition%20-%20Understanding%20Tubefeeding%202005.pdf.
23. Quoted in Cystic Fibrosis Foundation. "Supporting Nutrition."
24. Cystic Fibrosis Foundation. "Airway Clearance Techniques." www.cff.org/treatments/Therapies/Respiratory/AirwayClearance.
25. Thomson and Harris. *The Facts*, p. 43.

26. Jacqui Cowlard, Janelle Yorke, and Siobhan Carr. "Understanding Adolescents' Adherence to Their Cystic Fibrosis Treatments." Cystic Fibrosis Worldwide. www.cfww.org/pub/english/cfwnl/12/672/Understanding_Adolescents%E2%80%99_adherence_to_their_cystic_fibrosis_treatments.

27. Markovich. *Cystic Fibrosis Handbook for Patient and Family*, p. 37.

28. Quoted in Markovich. *Cystic Fibrosis Handbook for Patient and Family*, p. 118.

29. Quoted in Russell and Russell. *With Every Breath*, pp. 55–56.

30. Quoted in Thomson and Harris. *The Facts*, p. 34.

Chapter Four: Living with Cystic Fibrosis

31. Quoted in Russell and Russell. *With Every Breath*, pp. 34–35.

32. Quoted in Cystic Fibrosis Foundation. "CF Research Shows Importance of Mental Health." www.cff.org/About CFFoundation/Publications/connections/archive/September 2010/CF-Research-Shows-Importance-of-Mental-Health.cfm.

33. Quoted in Thomson and Harris. *The Facts*, p. 81.

34. Lauren Bombardier. "The Power of Positivity." Children's Hospital Cystic Fibrosis Center. http://childrenshospital.org/clinicalservices/Site1863/Documents/Laurens%20story.doc.

35. Quoted in CF Living. "Patient Stories." www.cfliving.com/resources/patient-stories.jsp.

36. Quoted in Cystic Fibrosis Foundation. "Going to College with CF." www.cff.org/AboutCFFoundation/Publications/connections/December2011/Going-to-College-with-CF.cfm.

37. Quoted in Russell and Russell. *With Every Breath*, pp. 40–41.

38. Cystic Fibrosis Foundation. "Cystic Fibrosis in the Workplace." www.cff.org/UploadedFiles/LivingWithCF/InWorkplace/CFInTheWorkplace.pdf.

39. Russell and Russell. *With Every Breath*, p. 66.

40. Quoted in Cystic Fibrosis Foundation. "The CF Balancing Act." www.cff.org/AboutCFFoundation/Publications/connections/archive/JulyAugust2009/The-CF-Balancing-Act.cfm.

41. Thomson and Harris. *The Facts*, p. 45.

42. Bob Esparza. "Bob's Story." Boomer Esiason Foundation. http://esiason.org/thriving-with-cf/story-archive/bob-esparza .php.

43. Quoted in Cystic Fibrosis Canada. "We Had Never Heard of Cystic Fibrosis Prior to That Day." www.cysticfibrosis.ca/en/ aboutCysticFibrosis/personalstories_LovisaMcCallum.php.

44. Boomer Esiason Foundation. "Letter from the Chairman." http://esiason.org/about-us/letter-from-the-chairman.php.

45. Quoted in Patrick Williams. "Mothers Have Hope for Cure." *Coolum News* (Coolum Beach, Australia), May 4, 2012. www.coolum-news.com.au/story/2012/05/04/mothers-have-hope-for-cure-cystic-fibrosis.

Chapter Five: The Future

46. Clinical Trials.gov. "CFfone: A Cell Phone Support Program for Adolescents with Cystic Fibrosis." http://clinicaltrials.gov /ct2/show/NCT01183286?recr=Open&cond=%22Cystic+Fibro sis%22&rank=69.

47. Canadian Cystic Fibrosis Foundation. "Hope Through Progress: Clinical and Scientific Research Programs, 2010–2011." www.cysticfibrosis.ca/assets/files/pdf/CCFF _clinical_n_Scientific_programsE.pdf.

48. Children's Hospital Boston. "Microbial Community Composition and Metabolism in Cystic Fibrosis." Clinical Trials.gov, August 5, 2009. http://clinicaltrials.gov/ct2/show /NCT00954018?recr=Open&cond=%22Cystic+Fibrosis%22& rank=63.

49. Cystic Fibrosis Foundation. "Learn About Clinical Trial Participation." www.cff.org/GetInvolved/ParticipateInAClinical Trial.

50. Quoted in Andrew Pollack. "Cystic Fibrosis Drug Gets Closer to Market." *New York Times*, February 24, 2011. http://health.nytimes.com/health/guides/disease/cystic-fibrosis /news-and-features.html.

51. Papworth Hospital. "Ghrelin in Cystic Fibrosis (Ghrelin)." Clinical Trials.gov, July 26, 2010. http://clinicaltrials.gov/ct2/show /NCT00763477?recr=Open&cond=%22Cystic+Fibro sis%22& rank=5.

52. Emory University. "Vitamin D for Enhancing the Immune System in Cystic Fibrosis (DISC Study)." Clinical Trials.gov, August 30, 2011. http://clinicaltrials.gov/ct2/show/NCT0142 6256?recr=Open&cond=%22Cystic+Fibrosis%22& rank=22.

53. Quoted in Robert Sanders. "'Evolved' Virus May Improve Gene Therapy for Cystic Fibrosis." *UC Berkeley News*, February 17, 2009. http://berkeley.edu/news/media/releases /2009/02/17_schaffer.shtml.

54. Quoted in Cystic Fibrosis Foundation. "One on One: Marc and Margarete Cassalina." www.cff.org/ECommitment/2007 _fall/people/one_on_one-marc_and_margarete_cassalina.html.

55. Quoted in Carolyn Sayre. "Cystic Fibrosis: Complicated and Variable." *New York Times*, April 24, 2009. www.nytimes .com/ref/health/healthguide/esn-cystic-fibrosis-expert.html.

56. Cystic Fibrosis Foundation. "About the Foundation." www .cff.org/AboutCFFoundation.

Glossary

acini: Cells in the pancreas that make digestive enzymes.

acute: Sudden onset.

airways: Tubes that carry air in and out of the lungs.

beta cells: Cells in the pancreas that make insulin.

biomarker: A chemical in the body that can be used to assess the presence or worsening of a disease.

bronchi: Airways connecting the windpipe and lungs.

carrier: A person who carries a gene mutation but does not develop a related disease.

channel: Tiny gate through which chemicals pass through cell walls.

chromosome: The wormlike body in the center of a cell where genes reside.

chronic: Long-term or ongoing.

cystic fibrosis: A disease characterized by thick, sticky mucus that prevents the lungs, pancreas, and other organs and glands from working properly.

cystic fibrosis transmembrane conductance regulator (CFTR): The cystic fibrosis transmembrane conductance regulator gene and the protein made by this gene.

digestive enzymes: Chemicals that help the body digest foods.

ducts: Tubes that carry secretions from exocrine glands.

epithelial cells: Cells that line the organs and glands affected by cystic fibrosis.

exocrine glands: Glands that secrete chemicals through ducts.

gene: The part of DNA that carries hereditary information.

genetic marker: Sequences of DNA that appear in families of people with certain genetic diseases.

huffing: Forced exhaling to free mucus trapped in the lungs.

insulin: A hormone secreted by beta cells in the pancreas, needed so cells can take in glucose.

ion: A charged atomic particle.

mucus: Fluid produced by epithelial cells in certain organs and glands.

nebulizer: A machine that converts a liquid medication to an inhalable form.

percussion: Clapping or thumping on the chest or back to free mucus from the lungs.

physiotherapy: Methods of draining mucus from the lungs and airways.

spirometry: Tests of lung function performed with a spirometer (a machine that measures how well a person breathes into a mouthpiece).

sputum: Mucus that has been coughed up from the lungs.

vector: A carrier that brings genes into cells in gene therapy.

ventilator: Also called a respirator; a machine that breathes for a patient who cannot breathe on his or her own.

Organizations to Contact

Cystic Fibrosis Foundation (CFF)
6931 Arlington Rd., 2nd Fl.
Bethesda, MD 20814
Phone: (301) 951-4422; toll-free (800) 344-4823
Website: www.cff.org

The CFF is the largest national nonprofit organization dedicated to supporting and educating patients and families and to funding CF research. It provides information on all aspects of the disease.

Cystic Fibrosis Research Inc. (CFRI)
2672 Bayshore Pkwy., Ste. 520
Mountain View, CA 94043
Phone: (650) 404-9975
Website: www.cfri.org

The CFRI is a nonprofit organization that funds CF research and provides education and support for patients and families.

Cystic Fibrosis Worldwide (CFWW)
210 Park Ave., #267
Worcester, MA 01609
Phone: (508) 762-4232
Website: www.cfww.org
The CFWW is an international nonprofit organization dedicated to promoting and supporting care for people with CF all over the world.

Cystic Life
3915 E. Broadway Blvd., Ste. 400
Tucson, AZ 85711
Website: http://cysticlife.org

Cystic Life is an online community that uses chats, blogs, profiles, and educational resources to allow members to exchange information and support.

National Heart Lung and Blood Institute (NHLBI)
NHLBI Health Information Center
PO Box 30105
Bethesda, MD 20824-0105
Phone: (301) 592-8573
Website: www.nhlbi.nih.gov

The NHLBI is the branch of the National Institutes of Health that conducts and funds research and provides public information on diseases such as CF that affect the lungs.

For More Information

Books

Melanie Ann Apel. *It Happened to Me: Cystic Fibrosis; The Ultimate Teen Guide.* Lanham, MD: Scarecrow, 2006. Based on interviews with teens and families affected by CF, this book offers insight into how teens live well with the illness and cope with its challenges.

Sharon Giddings. *Genes & Disease: Cystic Fibrosis.* New York: Chelsea House, 2009. This book written for teens focuses on the genetic causes of cystic fibrosis; it also discusses the history, treatments, and research.

Jacqueline Langwith. *Perspectives on Diseases and Disorders: Cystic Fibrosis.* Detroit: Greenhaven, 2008. This book for teens contains essays on all aspects of CF, including symptoms, causes, treatments, and research.

Jillian Powell. *Explaining: Cystic Fibrosis.* London: Franklin Watts, 2009. This book discusses history, causes, diagnosis, treatment, living with CF, and research in an easy-to-understand format.

Internet Sources

Mary Elizabeth Dallas. "Smoking's Effect on Lungs Similar to Cystic Fibrosis: Study." Health Day News. http://consumer.healthday.com/Article.asp?AID=657838.

Fox News. "Teen Discovers Promising Cystic Fibrosis Treatment." May 13, 2011. www.foxnews.com/health/2011/05/13/teen-discovers-promising-cystic-fibrosis-treatment.

Mayo Clinic. "Cystic Fibrosis." www.mayoclinic.com/print/cystic fibrosis/DS00287/DSECTION=all&METHOD=print.

National Heart Lung and Blood Institute. "What Is Cystic Fibrosis?" www.nhlbi.nih.gov/health/health-topics/topics/cf.

Websites

Claire's Place Foundation (http://clairesplacefoundation.org). Teenager Claire Wineland miraculously survived life-threatening complications of CF in 2010 and set up a foundation to help others with the disease. Her blog and videos have inspired countless people.

Cystic Fibrosis, TeensHealth from Nemours (http://kids health.org/teen/diseases_conditions/digestive/cystic_fibrosis .html). The nonprofit Nemours Foundation teen website provides information on all aspects of CF, including living with the illness.

Fitting CF into Your Life Everyday, Starlight Foundation (www.starlight.org/cf). Teens with CF helped set up this interactive program to help other teens and preteens learn to manage the disease. The program also offers an interactive question-and-answer section.

Gene Therapy and Children, KidsHealth from Nemours (http://kidshealth.org/parent/system/medical/gene_therapy .html). Provides an overview of the potential of gene therapy to cure diseases such as CF.

It's All About U, CF Voice (www.cfvoice.com/info/teens/index .jsp). A website where teens with CF can interact and share information and hope.

Index

Picture Credits

Cover: © MedicalRF.com/Alamy
© 3D4Medical/Photo Researchers, Inc., 17
© AJPhoto/Photo Researchers, Inc., 65
© AP Images/Idaho Statesman, Chris Butler, 79
© AP Images/Michael Brody, 81
© AP Images/PRNewsFoto/Advanced Respiratory Inc., 52
© Blend Images/Alamy, 42
© BSIP/Photo Researchers, Inc., 20, 22
© crozstudios/Alamy, 27
© Deco/Alamy, 36
© Du Hai/Xinhua/Landov, 33
© Dung Vo Trung/Sygma/Corbis, 41
© Gale/Cengage Learning, 26, 43
© Geoff Tompkinson/Photo Researchers, Inc., 83
© John Thys/Reporters/Photo Researchers, Inc., 9, 47
© Joubert/Photo Researchers, Inc., 13
© Martin Shields/Alamy, 90
© Mathieu Belanger/Reuters/Landov, 76
© Medical-on-Line/Alamy, 46
© Michael Donne/Photo Researchers, Inc., 87
© Peter Menzel/Photo Researchers, Inc., 71
© Phanie/Photo Researchers, Inc., 24, 39
© Publiphoto/Photo Researchers, Inc., 49
© Realimage/Alamy, 66
© Sheila Terry/Photo Researchers, Inc., 50
© Simon Fraser/Photo Researchers, Inc., 64
© Simon Fraser/RVI, Newcastle upon Tyne/Photo Researchers, Inc., 68
© Steve Gschmeissner/Photo Researchers, Inc., 57
© Tek Image/Photo Researchers, Inc., 30
© Véronique Burger/Photo Researchers, Inc., 60
© Yoon S. Byun/The Boston Globe via Getty Images, 89

About the Author

Melissa Abramovitz is the author of over thirty nonfiction educational books for children and teens. She has also published several children's picture books and hundreds of magazine articles for children, teens, and adults. Her book for writers of children and teen nonfiction was published in 2012.